Hadrian's Wildlife

John Miles

Hadrian's Wildlife

Whittles Publishing

Published by
Whittles Publishing Ltd.,
Dunbeath,
Caithness, KW6 6EG,
Scotland, UK

www.whittlespublishing.com

© 2012 John Miles

Main cover image © 2011 Matthew Lazzarini - lazz.smugmug.com

ISBN 978-184995-063-3

Printed by
Ashford Colour Press Ltd

Contents

I would like to dedicate this book to Paul Beniams (1956–2011) who would have helped me with it, but sadly left this earth. He loved, and worked, on the Wall.

Introduction

Hadrian's Wildlife might seem, to some, a strange title for a book. To me, though, it brings together two of the key elements of a landscape which I first came to know in 1981 as a warden for the RSPB based at Geltsdale: its man-made history and its natural history. Hadrian's Wall is a UNESCO World Heritage Site, rightly protected for future generations to admire. I believe that the landscape and the wildlife around the Wall deserve just as much protection.

The Roman emperor Hadrian ordered the building of the Wall in 122 A.D. as a defensive system to protect the English part of his empire. General Wade, leading a dash to Carlisle to defeat the Jacobite rebellion of 1745, poured Roman quarried stone in to the new road needed by his troops, not stopping to think that he was damaging a future tourist attraction. And neither did that trouble the many farmers who added Roman stone to their buildings because it was, well, only a stone's throw away from where they wanted to build. What you see today, then, are merely the remains of Hadrian's Wall.

The crumbling red sandstone on the western approaches was no match for the hard whin sill running through the central belt. The narrowest part of Britain was an ideal location in which to build a wall. The Romans had no idea that this was also already well known to the birds on migration which used it to cross from the Irish Sea to the North Sea.

My work in the area took off when it was felt that the RSPB should expand its woodland area to add to the 12,000 acres of mainly moorland to which it already had access, although it did not manage them. This brought me into contact with the Wall in several ways. The Lower Gelt woods owned by Brampton Parish Council are away from the Wall but had a quarry where the Romans excavated stone and left their mark in the crumbling 'Written Rock of Gelt'. The main inscription read, 'Vexillatio legionis secundæ ob virtutem appellatæ, sub agricola optione, apro et maximo, consulibus, oficina, mercati, mercatius ferni'. This translates as, 'The century of Julius Peculiaris: detatchment of the Twentieth Legion Valeria Victrix' (which was the legion that did much of the Wall construction.) However, another inscription refers to 'the consulship of Aper and Maximus, the working face of Mercatius' which dates from AD 207 showing that the quarry was in use over a long period. This was added to the reserve by lease, as were all the rest of the new woodland areas. Some of these are no longer part of the reserve but there may be public access.

Comb Crag, on the Wall itself, was – and is – an amazing piece of woodland with an ancient heath, also on sandstone and also close by a quarry used by the Romans. The new Hadrian's Wall Trail goes through the wood in its flatter section, the wood having survived only because its slopes prevent farmers and foresters from tearing its heart out. A small section of ancient oak survives at its eastern end, with bilberry as its main ground cover.

Another wood on the Irthing, called Quarry Beck, was acquired along with Boothby Bank near Lanercost. Here we look over the inspiring Lanercost Priory with its rich medieval history, the Wall running high above the river banks.

Areas of woodland looked at, but not added, to the reserve included Birdoswald, which was left to Cumbria County Council by the Henley family from Scaleby Castle, thought to have been built with red sandstone taken from the Wall. Irthing Gorge is now part of a Woodland Trust reserve famous for Sir Walter Scott and the Popping Stone.

These were the areas which I often used to visit but the Wall itself always tempted me to travel along it. The Military Road would take me off to the north-east coast to look for birds and other wildlife, while the sites along the Wall itself would see me enjoying the sheer experience of walking in Roman country.

I left the RSPB in 1991 and in 1992 wrote a book called Hadrian's Birds, a forerunner of this one and a taster of what people visiting the Wall could find in the region. The Wall was made into a World Heritage Site in 1987 and a lot of money has been spent on encouraging tourists to visit. The Hadrian's Wall Path was opened in 2004 and a cycle trail, National Route 72, passes through the area.

Farm agreements have been made to cover the management of land towards nature conservation and organisations like the RSPB and the National Trust have taken the lead in encouraging farmers and other landowners to protect wildlife on the farm. This has had an effect along the Wall and in the surrounding area, allowing habitats to be managed in a more sensitive way and encouraging wildlife to return. Furthermore, land has been bought purely in order to manage it for wildlife, with RSPB Campfield and RSPB Geltsdale serving as good examples at the west end, with Shibton Pond and the Rising Sun Country Park in the east. This book, like its predecessor, will start in the west and move east.

Acknowledgements

I would like to thank the following people for their help in this book: Mike Henry for his art work, Derrick Yalden for sourcing the Roman birds, Clive Griffiths for many trips around the Wall [photo of Waxwing], Steve Westerberg, Ian Ryding, Brian Little, Tony Lightly, Ewan Miles [photo of Hallbankgate], David Hickson [photo of Roe Deer and Hoverfly], Rob Shaw [photo of Banded Demoiselle and Barn Owl], Terry Pickford [photo of White Tailed Eagle], Mike Jackson, Steve Hewitt, Jeremy Roberts, Steve Lowe, Gill Thompson, Mick Simpson, James Littlewood, Tim Evans, Mark Newsome, Diana de Palacio, Colin Farquharson, Tyne Riverside Country Park staff and not forgetting my wife, Thelma, for her support.

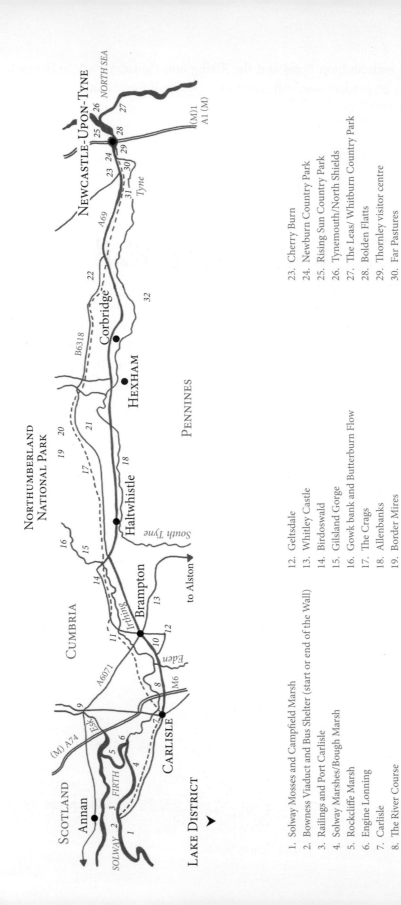

1. Solway Mosses and Campfield Marsh
2. Bowness Viaduct and Bus Shelter (start or end of the Wall)
3. Railings and Port Carlisle
4. Solway Marshes/Bough Marsh
5. Rockcliffe Marsh
6. Engine Lonning
7. Carlisle
8. The River Course
9. Netherby and Longtown
10. Written Rock of Gelt
11. Lanercost

12. Geltsdale
13. Whitley Castle
14. Birdoswald
15. Gilsland Gorge
16. Gowk bank and Butterburn Flow
17. The Crags
18. Allenbanks
19. Border Mires
20. Broomlea Lough
21. Grindon Lough
22. Whitley Dean

23. Cherry Burn
24. Newburn Country Park
25. Rising Sun Country Park
26. Tynemouth/North Shields
27. The Leas/ Whitburn Country Park
28. Bolden Flatts
29. Thornley visitor centre
30. Far Pastures
31. Rayton Meadows
32. Derwent Reservoir

The birds on the Wall

Standing on the Wall, looking out across the landscape, it is hard not to wonder what it would have been like to stand there when it was first built. Along the Wall today there is no shortage of information about the Romans and where their soldiers came from. Visitors can see artefacts like Roman shoes, they can visit the remains of Roman bath houses, stables and military quarters, even read letters from legionaries to their loved ones back home in places like North Africa and Bulgaria – yet there is not a single sentence about the landscape these people would have surveyed.

1

Bath house, Chesters

One thing, though, can give us an insight: bird remains. Certain birds needed certain habitats, as they do today, but game birds not only showed the importance of certain habitats, they were also food for the people living along the Wall. The four main species – capercaillie, grey partridge, black grouse and red grouse – have distinct habitats and could have lived around the Wall at this time.

The commonly-known pheasant was not yet present in the wild at the time of the Romans. This bird arrived from Asia and was named after the River Phasis in what is now called Georgia. The Latin name (*Phasianus colchicus*) also refers to the Colchis region in Georgia. The bird was first known in captivity in Egypt by 145–116 B.C. although the Greeks knew of it before this date. Pheasants would have been domesticated like the jungle fowl we use as poultry (hens or bantams) today, producing eggs as well as meat for the pot.

Capercaillie are found in coniferous forest, limited in Britain at that time to one species of tree, the Scots pine. This country was still recovering from the last Ice Age so Scots pine was once found from the south coast, moving north as the ice retreated, and already becoming edged out by broadleaved species which dominated, especially on the low ground. The last remaining wild woods of this species were found high on the Pennines and on outcrops in the Lake District south of the Wall, and to the north in the Caledonian Forest. Although capercaillie remains have been found at many Roman sites, especially York and, still closer to the Wall, at Durham, this bird's remains were absent from the Wall even as late as the 10th century.

The grey partridge is a species of open grassland and in particular of land under cultivation. The spread of this bird is a sign of early farming, clearing the land to grow crops and keeping domesticated animals and birds. It is the most common game bird found in digs around southern Roman Britain, but not here. It might have been expected to colonise the area once the Wall and its settlements had been established and trees around the Wall removed, but there are no records along the Wall. Equally, while the grey partridge also uses sand dunes, a habitat found at both ends of the Wall, there are no records in the settlements along its length.

The red grouse is common today because vast areas of moorland and upland are managed purely on its behalf. Again, it might be expected that this species would be very commonly found in digs around the Wall, but only one record has ever been found, from Corbridge, just south of the Wall. Does this mean that these vast tracts of open heather moorland did not exist? But what about the raised lowland bogs like Wedholme Flow and the Solway Mosses where red grouse bred until the 20th century? Surely these were open, given the vast amount of water kept in the peat? Where are the records of red grouse? It seems that these bogs were mostly covered in trees, some as much as 80%. Even before the Roman period, red grouse were found as remains further north and south of the Wall, suggesting more heather well away from the Wall. One site on the Wall which did have heather was Brocolitia, a word meaning 'heather fort'.

One of the problems heather faces is that it is classed as a temporary species in most of its range as its seed cannot germinate under the parent plant. What normally happens is that the heather plant becomes ragged and straggly, allowing other plants to come in and grow through it, creating a new habitat. The most common plants are trees like birch and, where found, Scots pine. One modern example of the recovery of heather was at Comb Crag near Birdoswald. A larch plantation blew down and was clear felled. No heather was found in the area but dormant heather seed sprang up to cover the ground, only for birch to seed through the heather, laying it dormant again.

Finally we come to the last species, the black grouse. Up until the 18th century this was the most common game bird in this area, as it had been in Roman times. In one paper, black grouse bones were described as being as common as those of domestic fowl. So what was the habitat which this species needed? The answer: scattered birch trees with berry-bearing scrub and shrubs and open areas of rough grassland and heath. Even deep in the peat today the birch tree dominates the fibre found in most areas.

Large amounts of timber will have been felled to build the Wall and the settlements associated with it. This will have encouraged new growth of birch, as this tree is described as a 'pioneer', meaning that it is often the first tree to colonise an area as its seed is transported by the wind. In contrast, the oak needs another species to carry its acorns away from the parent tree, the jay being the bird often associated with this task in this country.

Amazingly, no records of the jay from this period have ever been found further north than York. The world distribution of the jay takes it right across Europe into Russia, so it is doubtful that this bird was absent from the Wall. The modern Walton ('Wall Town') Moss has acorns planted all over it by jays.

A fifth game bird, the ptarmigan, was a lover of Arctic habitats. As the glaciers retreated, it was again pushed north by the progress of warming, which brought about a change in vegetation, and left its habitat only on the high mountains of Britain and not around the Wall. It would have become scarce even in the Lake District on sites like Skiddaw and Scafell where it became extinct as late as the 1800s. No records have been found for this bird in digs around the Wall, probably because its low numbers made it uneconomic to hunt.

Other influences on which bird species are found in digs along the Wall must include trade and the ability to catch the birds. If a species like red grouse was hard to catch before the invention of the gun, then this may well be the reason why so few examples have been discovered in digs.

3

The best description of the skills needed to catch birds is laid out in a volume by MacPherson written in 1897, called *A History of Fowling*. In this he describes how a thousand snares were placed out on a heather moor to capture a quarry. There are also descriptions of decoys, used to encourage cock red grouse to try and drive off the intruder on its territory, with clap nets used to capture the birds. All these devices would have been available to the locals in Roman times. The famous Vindolanda letters, written around 100 A.D. and found in 1973 by Robin Birley, even had a Flavius Cerialis writing, 'If you love me, brother, send me hunting nets.' The drag net will have been used for grey partridge, woodcock and, on short heath, red grouse, if it was present along the Wall.

Both snaring and clap netting were used on black grouse but not the decoy bird, as the black grouse is not a territorial bird, preferring instead to display in a lek. This is a display ground on which several males gather to display, the female mating with the bird she feels is dominant and going on to bring up her chicks on her own. This is also the method preferred by the capercaillie but not the red grouse nor the grey partridge. In these species, the cock holds an individual territory with both parents looking after their young in this well-defended area.

Trade was another reason behind the moving of a species from one area to another but this still did not bring large numbers of red grouse or grey partridge records to the Wall, although grey partridge was the most common game bird eaten at other Roman sites. Cultivation around the Wall to feed the army and its horses – Chesters being the best example of a cavalry fort in Britain – would have encouraged both partridge and black grouse, but still there are no remains of grey partridge.

At Vindolanda, 1,500 acres fed 500 soldiers. This would work out at 700 acres of cereal with the rest as grassland and woodland for 200 oxen, 200 ponies and pigs using the woodland. This would help to convince us that the habitat indeed consisted of scattered birch woodland with scrub, open grassland, heath and cultivation. These open areas would also be used by grazing red deer, with many bones found in Roman digs, especially at Carlisle and South Shields.

Domestic ponies would have been used by the British tribes for transport and war before the Romans came, and cattle would have provided meat and milk. As a defence system, large areas of trees may well have been felled in order to see any invader approaching the Wall, but as long as grazing was not too heavy the habitat would be used by black grouse. It has also been suggested that once the huge earthwork known as the Vallum was built behind the Wall, less grazing would have taken place to the north of the Wall due to the lack of access through the Vallum and the Wall for the local graziers.

Another example of the need of birch for black grouse was demonstrated during the very hard winter of 2009–2010. The numbers of black grouse on

Vindolanda

upland managed for red grouse dropped by 66% due to a lack of food and trees, while the numbers of black grouse with the right habitat, which included plenty of birch, actually increased. Some areas north of the Wall were thought to be re-established with trees on cultivated land due to the local tribes being driven away by the Roman invasion. This would also have helped the black grouse to expand.

Taking all this information into account, it would seem that the habitat on many sections of the Wall consisted of a mixture of cultivation, hay fields, rough grassland, heath, scrub and birch woodland.

The birch tree and scrub could not dominate in some habitats due to natural conditions. These included mature woodland, estuary, marshes and lakes, of which the Wall has its fair share. Starting with the estuaries, the Wall was built across the shortest crossing across Britain from east to west, both starting and finishing at an estuary. Nowadays these two estuaries are totally different, the Tyne being deep water and narrow while the Solway is very shallow and wide. At this time, though, both were deep enough to allow the type of boats used in the Roman period to arrive at the major cities of Carlisle, Corbridge and Newcastle. History shows us that Carlisle (current population 68,000) silted up while Newcastle (current population of more than half a million) became a centre of shipbuilding.

The two differ in terms of bird remains as well, with wild geese dominating at Carlisle. The Solway has always been a great place for wild geese, with a modern-day winter population of barnacle, pink-footed and greylag geese. Greylags even breed here, especially along the River Eden. A common breeding site for these geese was on the sandstone crags, as seen today along the River Eden. A place name south of here, Gaisgill, meaning 'goose ravine', proves that this type of nest site was used long ago.

Geese would have been caught using clap nets and trade will have taken them along the Wall with remains of barnacle goose being found at Vindolanda and even at York. Barnacle goose is a common wintering bird in Holland and some hard winters may have pushed the species to the Humber and closer to York. Three more species were found in Roman digs at Carlisle including brent, white-fronted and bean geese, none of which are regular visitors there today.

Up until the 1970s, bean geese were found along the Wall at Grindon Lough. A more recent arrival to that area has been a small number of Greenland white-fronted geese. Heavy grazing by domestic stock is thought to have removed the bean goose from that area as well as from an area by Castle Douglas in Dumfries and Galloway, close to the Solway.

The history of geese from Newcastle, on the other hand, is very patchy. Light-bellied brent geese are now found around Holy Island to the north, along with pink-footed geese around Druridge Bay. There is an interesting record of an estuarine bird, the shelduck, common on the Solway and to the north of Newcastle at Druridge Bay, found inland at Vindolanda. This may have been the result of trade or of the bird's moult migration as shelduck have only recently, in the last 30 years, moved inland to breed with birds now moving up the River Tyne and the River Eden.

Other ducks included mallard, wigeon and teal, all found around digs in Carlisle and present in large numbers today on the Solway, while wigeon and teal can be found in big numbers to the north of Newcastle at Holy Island and inland at Grindon Lough, close to Housesteads. All three species could have bred in the area of the Wall, with wigeon preferring to nest in colonies of black-headed gulls for protection from predators.

Estuaries are well known for their wintering wading birds and again the Solway would have had the bulk of these birds. Present-day records of thousands of lapwing and golden plover remind us of the remains of golden plover found at Carlisle, while Newcastle records may well have come from St Mary's, just north of the Tyne, where birds can be found today. Both these birds could have bred during Roman times, with golden plover preferring open short-turf upland while lapwing would use the estuaries as well as short-turf lowland. The size of the field systems at this time may have been too small for lapwing to use compared with today's large fields.

Other waders found at digs at Roman sites around England include grey and ringed plover, dunlin, snipe, bar-tailed and black-tailed godwit, whimbrel, curlew, redshank, greenshank and knot. All these winter in, or pass through, the Solway and Tyne area. The turnstone is more common on the Tyne due to its rocky shore compared to the mud and sand of the Solway.

The Wall has its fair share of freshwater marshes, many of which are associated with larger areas of standing water. Common cranes used to breed during Roman times and may well have bred along the Wall. They were eaten by the Romans and even gave their name to place names, especially during medieval times. Remains were found at Carlisle, Vindolanda, Housesteads, Corbridge and at Papcastle near Cockermouth. Even the ancient Egyptians would harvest these birds and house them for later eating, as seen on the great wall paintings in the tombs.

The main breeding habitat for common cranes in Europe is raised bog, a habitat found along the Wall. On such bogland one of their favourite foods is cranberry, misspelt now but originally 'craneberry'.

Whooper swans are a winter visitor, mainly from Iceland. Their habitat was once the many lakes, tarns and loughs found along the Wall. Remains have been found both at Carlisle and Vindolanda. Modern farming practices, with large areas of winter wheat sown in the autumn and constant feeding by the Wildfowl and Wetlands Trust at Caerlaverock by the Solway, has limited the use of these waters by this species. Mute swans, on the other hand, are territorial and individual pairs will protect a stretch of water from intruders. The third swan, the Bewick's swan, was found in digs at York but not along the Wall. A wintering site for this bird at York was the neighbouring Derwent Ings, where they are still found today. The Geordie naturalist Thomas Bewick (see separate chapter), famous for his woodcuts, gave his name to this bird so they were certainly found in the Northumbria area in the 18th century.

One wader which reflects the presence of woodland is the woodcock. It can breed in conifer or broadleaved woodland and is also a migrant from Europe in winter. It was found at digs in Carlisle and is the most common wader found around the Roman digs elsewhere. It is well known for its fine flavour.

Other woodland nesting birds would have been birds of prey. Both red kite and white-tailed eagle have been found in digs at Carlisle, and both could have been scavenging around the settlements. The red kite has been reintroduced to an urban area recently at Gateshead after disappearing due to persecution by game-rearing interests, and will hopefully spread along the Wall for all to enjoy. The white-tailed eagle is slowly making its way south after also being removed by landowners and game-rearing interests. Other birds of prey whose remains have not been found along the Wall but which are common in Roman digs elsewhere are buzzard and kestrel. Steel Rigg has the largest cliff in the area and both golden eagle and peregrine falcon may have nested here before the Wall was built.

Other scavenging species include raven, crow and jackdaw, all found at Carlisle, with both raven and crow found inland at Vindolanda. Ravens and crows can nest in trees as well as on crags, while the jackdaw needs holes in trees or crags. Two villages around Carlisle were named Great Corby (Raven) and Little Corby after the crow. Owls were represented by barn, long-eared and short-eared, but no records of tawny owl have been found at this time in Roman Britain, even though they have been found earlier and later in ancient digs. One theory is that they had not adapted to human settlements by this time, while the barn owl was named for its use of a man-made structure.

Owls have an interesting history with the Romans. For 500 years the Greeks had coins with the sacred little owl on one side, while Athena, the goddess of wisdom, linked wisdom to the owls. The Romans took Athena and turned her into Minerva, their god of wisdom along with Athena's owl but owls were already classed as evil creatures and symbols of death because they fly at night. The little owl is often seen hunting during the day and even that may not have saved it. An owl sitting on someone's house meant that death was on its way. The Romans thought witches could turn themselves into owls and that if an owl called, a witch was approaching. Owls were caught and killed and nailed to the house door to ward off this evil. Pliny the Elder wrote the first *Natural History* in 77 A.D. in which he noted that owls sitting on houses did not mean that people were going to die, but this book cannot have been a bestseller as the killing continued, regardless of the fact that fewer owls meant more rats and mice living in or around the house.

A lack of seabirds along the Wall seems to suggest there was little trade in these birds, given that Roman York was awash with them. Both sides of the Wall are close to sea cliffs for breeding, at St. Bees in Cumbria and the Farne Islands north of Newcastle, with more sea cliffs along the Solway in Dumfries and Galloway. A medieval record of Manx shearwater from Newcastle may suggest that this bird should have appeared along the Wall. Young would have been taken out of their burrow nesting sites for food, as a near relative from Australia is called the 'mutton bird' for its taste. The Manx name comes from the Isle of Man which

Long-eared owl

8

you can see from the west coast of Cumbria and Dumfries and Galloway, where the bird nests to this day.

The bones of a limited number of small birds – starling, dunnock and wagtail – at Carlisle and Birdoswald survived this period but the best site for preserved bones is Ossom's Eyrie Cave in the Peak District of Staffordshire. As the cave was well away from development through the ages, with no demolition of buildings or rebuilding on top of old structures, it kept bones high and dry. The name suggests the breeding site of the golden eagle ('erne' or 'heron' is often used for white-tailed eagle crag nesting sites) whose remains were found inside the cave. A wide range of birds was found, from thrushes and larks to buntings, even including spotted flycatcher and blue tit.

New digs around the country will add to the list of species found in Roman Britain, helped by a collection of modern bones to aid identification which has been put together at Southampton University. The present list of species stands at around half the number recorded today, but changes have been seen even in my lifetime, and new ones are likely thanks to future management along the Wall. The ebb and flow of migration, too, is always likely to send birds around the Wall.

9

Short-eared owl

The Solway estuary

Regardless of whether you start at the west or the east end of the Wall, the Solway is for the naturalist one of the splendours of this area. Bowness may mark the end of the Wall but the Solway stretches on down as far as St. Bees on the south side and up to the Mull of Galloway on the north side. The Romans knew this, as forts stretched down as far as Ravenglass, south of St. Bees, to add protection to the area from the 'barbarians' across on the north side of the Solway. Ravenglass is famous for having the tallest Roman wall still standing, part of the bath house situated in the fort called Glannaventa, built around 150 A.D.

Most of this south side of the Solway is very flat, with only St. Bees adding its great red sandstone cliffs, making it an attractive place for large numbers of sea-birds to nest. Here you can find guillemots, razorbills, kittiwakes, cormorants and small numbers of puffins and black guillemots. The flora is special, with wood- and horseshoe vetch, sea pink, scurvy grass and dyer's greenweed, to name just a few. Porpoise, dolphins and even whales can be spotted in summer, with grey seals all year round.

Harbours stretch back from Whitehaven to Silloth until the sands and mud of the Inner Solway become too shallow for most boats. From Silloth, a shingle arm sticks out into the Solway. This is Grune Point, with its breeding and wintering waders and geese and a migration hotspot for birds, both when moving off in spring and when returning from further north and east in the autumn. Plants like sea holly, marram grass and thick areas of gorse add to the occasion.

Back to Bowness, a great place to start the Wall with a raised mound to build the second largest fort along the Wall (Maia) and a great view across the surrounding area, with the hill of Criffel on the Scots side, the Pennines to the east and the Lake District fells to the south. The modern search for birds has made the site famous, this being one of the best places on the British mainland to watch for the sea passage of one family, the skuas.

With the Hadrian's Wall Path, which runs for 84 miles from Bowness to Wallsend, starting or finishing in what we call the 'bus shelter' (NY225628), it can get very busy here at times, especially in April and May, peak time for skuas in spring but less so in autumn. With telescopes pointing out into the channel, rucksacks and posing walkers (posing sweatily if they've just finished) wanting their photos taken, the shelter can get very crowded. It is questionable how many of these long-distance walkers look down onto the mosaic in the shelter. Here are several of the birds found on the Solway mimicking a Roman mosaic like the one found in the House of Birds at Italica near Seville.

The high ground offers a great view over this section of the Solway and with an incoming tide the birds are often driven into the estuary by a south-west wind.

Four species of skua can be found, the great skua often being the first to show. It has even wintered here, feeding on dead sheep washed down by the rivers. The Arctic skua is often next, with pomarine, the most common, appearing from early April to late May. The long-tailed skua is often limited to a two-week period in May. The autumn passage is never as strong but is still worth looking out for from as early as July through to October, when the Arctic skua is normally the most common.

The spring passage often sees birds travelling inland to cross the country at its shortest crossing into the North Sea. Thousands of kittiwakes have been counted, joined by divers and ducks. Strong winds can blow seabirds, like the ones nesting at St. Bees, into the estuary. Joining them are gannets, Manx shearwaters, Leach's and storm petrels and even little auks in winter.

A general movement of birds can result from displacement due to high tides or strong winds, which can affect birds like great crested grebes, red-throated divers, goldeneye and greater scaup, using the estuary to feed further out but moved by these tides. Rarer ducks and grebes can occur, with long-tailed duck and even velvet scoter. Eider is rare in these parts, as are Slavonian and red-necked grebe. The high tides can even move the geese, especially the barnacle geese feeding on Rockcliffe Marsh. Hundreds and sometimes thousands can fly past the shelter, heading for drier ground, often onto the Wildfowl and Wetlands Trust reserve at Caerlaverock on the Scottish side.

Some of my best encounters here have included the big storm of 23 May 2011 when over 60 long-tailed skuas flew into the Solway on a massive south-west wind. A group of 44 were first seen dancing over the waves as their light, tern-like flight struggled with the high winds. This group of birds stayed for an hour in the bay before rising high and travelling past the bus shelter. Walkers from Holland were amazed to find so many birdwatchers crammed into the shelter, with one asking if we were watching for a 'Scots invasion'. It was instead an invasion of birds, heading for the high Arctic. A further 120 long-tailed skuas were seen later in the week.

One amazing day brought an encounter with a female sparrowhawk. Only myself and my birding mate Clive were in the shelter for a spot of autumn watching. I was standing up close to the railing and Clive was sitting down. The bird flew between both of us with one wing brushing my jacket. It was probably in the habit of using the shelter as a flyway, trying to catch out an unsuspecting robin or blackbird as they darted along the track and through the shelter.

Tides will also disrupt the feeding and roosting of waders using the estuary, so species like oystercatcher, redshank, dunlin, ringed plover, bar-tailed and black-tailed godwit, golden plover and curlew can fly by. Gulls are always present somewhere here and feeding and going to roost means a continuous passage of lesser black-backed and herring gulls nesting on Rockcliffe Marsh, along with others like black-headed and common gulls, with the odd rarer birds such as Mediterranean, little and Iceland gull.

Another place from which to watch this movement is the old viaduct (NY212628). The viaduct has a painful history. Hard winters, like that of 2010–2011, can leave a lot of ice around the edges of the rivers and the estuary and by 1881, after just twelve years in service, the viaduct had been breached in two places by icebergs. With a thaw upstream, bergs measuring as much as ten feet thick and 27 feet square, tore at the structure, leaving the line in ruin. It was repaired but by 1934–1935, the main structure had been demolished.

What remains is a 440-yard sea embankment looking out into the estuary. This gives great views of the movement of birds but no shelter, so you are exposed to the wind, the rain and even the waves. Overall, though, it can be better than using the shelter, especially when porpoise hunt fish in the Solway or a grey seal pops up to have a look at you. The count of great crested grebes floating by on a flat calm tide can be in treble figures, while the cormorant never gives up trying to swallow that 'flatty'.

My early memories of birding here include 14 black terns flying out of the estuary and briefly landing right in front of us. That is a very good count for a bird which does not breed in Britain and is very uncommon in Cumbria. I have witnessed Pomarine skuas floating by the end of the viaduct with their 'spoons' (tail streamers) flashing in the sun and hundreds of kittiwakes stooping and rising up, heading inland.

To the east of the shelter is a site called the Railings. This area can be used by roosting waders, especially in spring and autumn, with thousands often just feet away from you. They congregate first on the mud and, as the tide moves in, slowly make their way onto the shingle. Here you can find mainly ringed plover and dunlin but mixed in with them can be sanderling, turnstone, oystercatcher and redshank.

13

Over the years much rarer birds have been found, including broad-billed sandpiper and Kentish plover. In autumn, curlew sandpiper and little stint are much more common, often as juvenile birds. At low tide these birds feed out along the estuary, especially towards Port Carlisle (NY240623). This former port was established when the mud and sands prevented shipping from reaching Carlisle, but was then swallowed up in its turn, leaving a canal and a railway with nothing to service.

Someone's loss is always another's gain, though, and for the birds it serves as a great feeding area, bringing in grey heron and new species like little egret. The old harbour wall acts as a roost for the waders, especially for redshank and oystercatchers, but rarer birds like greenshank, spotted redshank, long-billed dowitcher, American golden plover and semi-palmated sandpiper have been found feeding on the mud. Common terns can nest in the area, with windswept Arctic and white-winged black terns resting here.

What remains of the canal is marked by the presence of phragmites or common reed. This tall plant will have colonised the canal after its demise, leaving the likes of sedge warblers to use its long stalks on which to build their nests. The reed is like heather, in that it cannot dominate an area and each year its remains build up in the water, allowing other plants, especially willow, to come in. Once the trees take over, the drying-out process takes place and more trees like alder and birch come in until there is a real dominance of oak and ash. And, like history, the wildlife moves on to another story.

Summer is also the time to see haaf netters trying to catch salmon and sea trout. This type of netting dates back to the Viking era and has managed to survive along the Solway. The normal view is of several men (I have never seen a woman) standing in line with poles to which are attached a net. The idea is that the changing tide carries the fish into the net before the pole is lifted and the fish removed, to be placed in a bag on the fisherman's back. Even porpoise and grey seals coming well into the Solway can push fish into the nets. Walkers following the Solway on the Hadrian's Wall Path may well see the haaf nets lying out to dry.

Grey heron

Barnacle geese

The Solway Mosses

The Solway Mosses is an area of around 5,500 acres of peat mires, mostly in the charge of Natural England. Formed from the last Ice Age, when the glaciers left shallow depressions which filled up with water, their edges grew sphagnum mosses, creating an acid habitat which prevented vegetation from decomposing. This formed the peat which acted as a sponge, holding water. This water prevented many species of plant from growing, allowing a limited community of heathers and even insect-eating plants to thrive.

16

2,500 acres of this area is called the South Solway Mosses, made up of Wedholme Flow (NY220530), Glasson (NY240600) and Bowness Common (NY200590). Only Wedholme Flow has been heavily worked for peat extraction and was bought out by Natural England in 2002 at a cost of £17.3 million, along with two other mosses in Yorkshire. Four hundred acres are being converted back to moss land, with flooded lagoons built into the open peat.

This area has been colonised by many breeding birds, with redshank, lapwing, snipe, curlew, teal, shelduck and even little ringed plover using the site. Passage waders like black-tailed godwit, ruff, dunlin, knot and avocet have been seen here. Gulls both breed and loaf or roost in the area. Wintering birds include roosting whooper swans in their hundreds, pink-footed geese, often in their thousands, mallard, teal, wigeon and shoveler.

The rest of the moss area is covered with common heather, with sphagnum mosses holding the water in the area. Other plants here include three species of sundew, which add insects to their menu to obtain the nutrients which the moss lacks, bog rosemary, cross-leaved heath, which likes wetter areas than heather, and cranberry. Pitcher plant from North America, another insect eater, was found at Wedholme but many have been removed as it is an alien species.

Bird species are somewhat restricted in these mosses, with red grouse now on its last legs and even hen harrier, which once hunted the area in summer, now restricted to winter and then mainly to roosting, having hunted around neighbouring farmland. Stonechat and whinchat enjoy the summer, along with meadow pipit and curlew. Mammals include foxes and roe deer, with adders basking in the open areas. Drumburgh Moss (NY255586) is just outside the village of Drumburgh and is the closest to the Wall itself. Short-eared and barn owl can be seen in winter.

The real prize of these mosses comes in the form of dragonflies, with several species using the wet hollows to breed and hunt over. Large emperor dragonflies dwarf the emerald damselfly, with up to 12 species found on most of these mosses.

Roe deer

Some of these hollows have been made by the domestic extraction of peat for burning on fires, but new water has often arrived due to the blocking up of drains once dug to try to make the land fit for agriculture. The drains are blocked in order to keep the moss wet and capture the carbon locked up in the peat. The wetter the moss, the more carbon will be held in place.

17

Set against this is the natural regeneration of trees which can reduce this water and dry out the mosses. Conservationists fight a constant battle to prevent woodland from taking over. Orton Moss (NY339543) is now mainly trees but has recently been bought by Cumbria Wildlife Trust, so management may well reduce the trees here. The remaining mosses, like Scaleby, just north of the Wall (NY430635), have a ring of birch and pines growing around the perimeter and always trying to move into the centre. Several attempts have been made to convert the moss to agricultural land, with parcels removed over the course of the century.

This moss (Scaleby) has one big rarity: the white-faced darter, a dragonfly restricted to a small number of sites throughout Britain. It has declined from southern Britain and is now found in these restricted sites from the Midlands to the Highlands of Scotland. Here at Scaleby, the regeneration of trees is drying out the moss and the oligotrophic bog pools which need sphagnum growth for the larvae to flourish.

One butterfly worth looking for is the large heath, not to be confused with its relative, the small heath, found along the Wall itself. Scaleby is very good for this butterfly from June to July, although it often falls prey to the many dragonflies around the moss. The wall butterfly was not named after this Wall but after all of them, as it often chooses to perch on a wall to get the full effect of the sun. This butterfly is commoner on low ground at either end of the Wall.

An unusual species not found widely in Cumbria is the tea tree (*Lycium europium*), thought to have been introduced from southern Europe, although not by the Romans. Adders are plentiful, as are common lizards, which often fall prey to the snakes. The removal of pines can also take away the food of the red squirrel which has been pushed into conifer plantations by the ever-increasing grey squirrel.

Three more mosses are found just north of the Wall, with Bolton Moss and Solway Moss both being worked for peat but with a limited life left, as Natural England has bought them in order to start a restoration programme. I visited Bolton Moss a few years ago and was amazed that the peat in the drainage ditches was between 12 and 15 feet in depth. The only birdlife found was the oystercatcher, while both curlew and lapwing nested in the surrounding fields. No vegetation was visible on the worked areas.

The Solway Moss (site of the Battle of Solway Moss in 1542) has now mostly been planted up with commercial forestry by the Netherby estate, the site of the Roman fort Castra Exploratorum. Species like lodgepole pine and sitka spruce, both originally natives of the west coast of North America, have been planted. The remaining area of peatworks does hold some areas of open water with several species of dragonflies present. The company working the moss were trying to speed up the growth of sphagnum to sell as floral background: using sphagnum this way prolongs the life of cut flowers as water is retained by the moss. The rest of the moss, like Bolton Moss, was pure exposed peat with only oystercatchers and lapwing using the area.

The Solway Moss also tells a story regarding the history of mosses generally. On the night of 16 November 1771 the tragedy known as the eruption of the Solway Moss occurred. Peat mosses act as a sponge soaking up water until they can hold no more and, on this night, 300 acres of peat exploded out of the 1,600 acres of moss and covered 400 acres of farmland. No one was killed but many cattle were lost, with 28 families losing their homes to the rush of peat and water. The peat was washed into the River Esk and later washed up on the shores of the Isle of Man. Several have erupted through their life around Britain and I am sure more will do so in the future.

Walton Moss (Wall Town) is covered in sphagnum with many species similar to Scaleby. Both black and red grouse were once found here and hen harrier and short-eared owl often winter here. The large daytime-flying emperor moth is common here, providing food for the cuckoo which enjoys the large caterpillars feeding on the heather. Both meadow and tree pipits attract the cuckoo to lay its egg in their nests, often concealed in the cotton grass which throws its head to the wind in May and June.

Lapwing chick

19

The Solway Marshes

Those who have walked the Wall will know the slog across Burgh Marsh. To some it is flat and boring, but to those with an eye and an ear, it is full of life. The old Wall here would have been a turf affair so the flood bank along the road may well have looked like it. The area would certainly have been much wetter and where you find water, you often find waders, especially in spring, displaying over these marshes.

Due to tidal flooding these marshes have never been reclaimed for intensive farming so stretching from Silloth you have Skinburness, Border, Newton, Cardurnock and Campfield Marsh before Bowness and Burgh and Rockcliffe and arrival at Carlisle. The main grazing animals are sheep and cattle, all removed when high tides come to the area. The outbreak of foot and mouth disease in 2001 left the marshes ungrazed for a period of time, allowing some plant species to flourish, especially sea pink, scurvy grass and sea aster. All the marshes are now protected from development by their Site of Special Scientific Interest status for their birds, flora and geology.

The largest of these marshes is Rockcliffe Marsh, cut off from most areas by the two rivers entering the Solway, the Esk and the Eden. This marsh holds around 4,000 acres of salt marsh with many natural creeks draining the land. The marsh itself has grown west into the Solway as sediments build up around its shore. These sediments are then held together by sea grasses like pucinelia, and other pioneering plants include sea milkwort.

Apart from this, there is a transition to grassy salt marsh dominated by red fescue, thrift and salt marsh rush. In places, creeping bent, sea plantain and sea arrow grass also occur. Larger areas of sea aster occur where the big gull colony prevents grazing by domestic stock in summer. Their seed is fed on in winter by both linnet and twite. Closer to the high tide mark are plants like soft rush and flowering rush. It was such a large area of flat land that the marsh was considered a possible German invasion landing area during World War Two, and large stakes were driven into the marsh to prevent gliders from landing.

The marsh has the largest population of breeding waders in Britain, with oystercatcher, curlew, ringed plover, redshank and lapwing. Former breeders included dunlin, ruff and black-tailed godwit, all of which can be seen in spring and autumn. A large gull colony is now found at the western tip of the marsh, containing lesser black-backed gulls and herring gulls, with several thousand of each species nesting. These birds used to nest on Wedholme Flow but moved here as it was safer and closer to food in Carlisle. Another large gull which has recently started nesting here is the greater black-backed gull. This bird is more common in winter as many come down from northern Scotland to feed on dying salmon.

A smaller gull, the black-headed gull, used to nest in its hundreds and in turn protected common and Arctic terns nesting here, keeping predators away. The black-headed gull's numbers have fallen and so have those of the terns, as the bigger gulls could sweep in and feed on their eggs and chicks. Several species of duck nest on these marshes: no-one could miss the brightly coloured shelduck. These birds nest in holes in the creek walls and in rabbit burrows and the females form crèches, gathering the young together as a way of protecting them from predators like the big gulls. So successful has the bird become at building its numbers here that adults now move upriver to breed inland. This bird also has an amazing moult migration, flying out to Germany where the Waddenzee mudflats offer a safe area for the birds to be flightless as they lose their wing feathers. Small groups of birds fly through the Tyne Gap during July, August and September, with groups grounded by bad weather seen at Tindale Tarn and Grindon Lough.

In winter the marsh becomes a sea of geese, with the population of Svalbard barnacle geese enjoying the rich sea grasses found here. Recent radio tagging of birds has shown that when the birds migrate north in the spring, every one of the radio-tagged birds has come to this marsh to fatten up for the long migration. This information is critical in protecting the marsh from over-zealous industrialists who want to flood the marsh with a barrage across the Solway.

The barnacle geese are often joined by thousands of pink-footed geese, hundreds of greylag geese and small numbers of rarer geese like snow, Ross's, brent and white-fronted. Many of these geese were hunted in Roman times, with bones found in Carlisle. Winter duck can include pintail, wigeon, mallard and teal, again often in large numbers.

These marshes are home to one of Britain's rare amphibians, the natterjack toad. They breed in small shallow pools, often by the side of the road, and Campfield Marsh is a good place to find them.

Much of Burgh Marsh can be viewed from the minor road between Burgh and Drumburgh, especially using the two high ridges along the road. To view other areas of the marsh, two public footpaths lead onto Burgh marsh, one starting at NY307592 and the other at NY329603. Edward I's monument is found here, erected after his death in 1307 as his armies used to cross into Scotland from this point. His nickname was Longshanks, so it is appropriate that he has a link with the redshanks and greenshanks on this marsh.

Rockcliffe Marsh can also be viewed from this point but closer views can be had from the Old Boat House at NY230628 or along the footpath at NY353619. The marsh itself is a Cumbria Wildlife Trust reserve and permits are needed to enter the site. Other marshes can be scanned from roads: Skinburness Marsh at NY137547 and Border Marsh at NY152523. Both these are crossed by the Cumbrian Coastal Way. Newton Marsh can be viewed from NY186521 and again from NY200583 in Anthorn. This minor road carries on round to Cardurnock and Campfield.

Buzzard

Above: A sericomyia silentis

Right: Allen banks

Above: Whinsill Woodland

Top left: Banded demoiselle

Middle left: Emperor moth

Bottom left: Elephant hawk-moth

Above: Barn owl in a box

Top right: Fog from the Tyne

Bottom right: Fungus

This page

Top right: Goldenrod

Middle: Painted lady

Bottom right: Northern marsh orchid

Opposite page

Top: Dryad's Saddle

Bottom: Globe flower on Gowk bank

Above: Red admiral

Top right: Poppy rape next to Chesters

Bottom right: Mosaic, Bowness

Campfield Marsh

Just outside Bowness is the RSPB reserve of Campfield Marsh (NY197615). This reserve was formerly bought for its marsh area where there is a regular wader roost in winter, while the farmland was there to encourage geese in winter. The name is evidence of yet another Roman camp which was found on the farm called Campfield, not part of this reserve.

As the Solway is one of the top estuaries in the UK for birdlife in particular, this reserve has much to offer. The reserve itself has its own farm at North Plain. It has two miles of coastline running right up to Bowness and about 150 acres of salt marsh, as well as about 1,250 acres of grassland and raised bog, part of Bowness Common. This offers wildlife a wide choice through the seasons. At present it has one hide, overlooking grassland, wetland and Bowness Common.

From January onwards the reserve comes into its own. The hide offers views over water which will not be there come May, when cattle are brought onto the reserve to graze the fields. This water backs up to birch woodland which is part of Bowness Common. As the water is very shallow it is ideal for dabbling ducks like mallard, teal, shoveler, pintail and wigeon. The pintail are quite rare along the Wall and over 100 can often be seen from here. The wigeon move out onto the grassland to graze the short turf while the rest are quite content to feed around the area.

Lapwing is the most common wader here, often joined by redshank, and both breed on the farm. Snipe and jack snipe, a winter visitor, use the rushes for cover, while curlew are often seen feeding out in the open. January and February also see the peak arrival of geese onto the reserve and the surrounding area. Pink-footed and barnacle often flock together to graze the fields around the farm. The hide often allows very close views of the geese.

Certain fields on the farm are used for 'cropping', the growing of a mixture of crops for seed for the farmland finches and buntings to enjoy. Numbers for these birds can be in the hundreds, with lots of reed buntings, yellowhammers, chaffinches and tree sparrows. These then encourage birds of prey to hunt here. One field is to the left of the hide so, sitting in comfort, you can scan the field waiting for birds of prey to come.

A highlight in recent years has been provided by hunting hen harriers. It is great to see them hunting just before they go to roost on the common. Recent sightings have demonstrated the differences in hunting technique between young and adult birds; young birds are likely to fly up and down the field, scaring the birds into thick hawthorn bushes, although this means that there will then be few birds to try to catch. Adults, on the other hand, make a sweep of the field before going to perch, allowing the birds time to emerge from the thorns and start feeding again. When the birds are settled, the adult will again try its luck, this time with a better chance of actually catching its prey. Species such as the sparrowhawk will also make the most of this disturbance to attack, often catching the birds off guard. All this makes for exciting viewing – unless you are a small bird, of course.

As spring approaches, the numbers of birds using the reserve increase, with new migrants arriving from as far away as Africa. Wheatears and sand martins are often the first to arrive, often being seen out on the salt marsh. Ospreys cross the reserve, heading for the short crossing of the Solway, followed by newly-arrived waders such as black-tailed godwit, ruff and whimbrel. White wagtails are joined by meadow pipits along with summer-plumaged waders on the salt marsh, with grey plover, bar-tailed godwit and knot making their way north.

Breeding gets underway with the lapwing, while tree sparrows and willow tits try out the many boxes erected for them down the lane to the hide. Sedge warblers and common whitethroats enjoy the thick hedges down the lane while both lesser whitethroat and grasshopper warblers are found around the thick gorse along the roadside.

Several rarer birds have been found over the years: red-backed shrike, ring-necked duck, common crane, spoonbill, great white egret, glossy ibis, green-winged teal and American wigeon. The bird that really brought in the crowds was a stilt sandpiper found on the salt marsh pool, while one that would have done so had it stayed was a white-tailed eagle from the east of Scotland release programme in Fife.

Natterjack toads can be heard in the springtime, using the pools dug for them along the salt marsh. Badgers even have their latrine along the track to the hide, while foxes and roe deer are frequently seen out on the common. Summer may lack birds but the numbers of dragonflies using the many ditches around the farm make up for them. Species include southern and migrant hawker, emperor and scarlet darter, which is a rare find from southern Europe.

Autumn sees the return of waders to the salt marsh, with several thousand oystercatchers, curlew, redshank, golden plover, dunlin, ringed plover and knot using the roosting site close to the salt marsh pool. All these waders attract birds of prey, especially the peregrine falcon. When they take flight together in a blur of wings, you know a falcon has come into the roost. Both sparrowhawk and merlin also hunt here, along with the occasional hen harrier. Geese tend not to feed close to the reserve on their return but often stay well away from the area, returning only once the shooting season is over.

With all this wildlife to watch, this makes a great location for a centre. I am sure the Romans would have been happy to see the Wall finish here.

Hunting Fox, sunny evening

Mike Henry
2011

Fox

The river course

The Wall has two main rivers – one to the west and one to the east. This section covers the one to the west: the River Eden which cuts through between Burgh and Rockcliffe Marshes, leaving the Solway behind. The tidal effect of the sea is evident beyond Rockcliffe village as flatfish like dabs enjoy the sandy bottom of the river, and salmon and sea trout make their way upriver to spawn.

Two cliffs are found in the village. The more impressive is the red sandstone cliff which rises above the river, offering nesting sites for stock dove and jackdaws and roosting sites for kestrel, barn owl and the occasional peregrine falcon. The other cliff is the river bank itself and where the soil is deep, large cliffs of sand are available for sand martins to dig their tunnel nests and raise their broods. The river acts as a cleaner for these birds, washing out the nests each winter, destroying many mites and fleas carried by the birds into their nesting holes and helping to ensure that the young are not bled to death by these parasites.

The red sandstone was used to build the Wall in this section, but very little is left to see as exposed stones left at the mercy of the elements have crumbled away. In some sections the Wall has been covered up to prevent this erosion. The Wall is found again at Kirkandrews with a great view upriver. Winter birds here include goosander and goldeneye, and even smew have been found. Whooper swans graze the fields in this area and are always flying around, heading back onto Rockcliffe Marsh.

A local nature reserve is found at Engine Lonning (NY382563) which was once a busy railyard for the London and North Eastern Railway. The railyard closed in the early 1960s and nature has been swift to reclaim the area. Carlisle City Council manages the area as part of its parks scheme. The area has a mixed covering of sycamore, ash, birch and both willow and hawthorn scrub. Bramble, ivy and fat hen add to the diversity, allowing large numbers of warblers to use the site in spring. Chiffchaff and both willow and garden warbler are joined by blackcap and common whitethroat. Open areas along the river have canary grass, allowing sedge warbler to breed.

The river walk through the Lonning forms part of both the Hadrian's Wall National Trail and the Cumbria Coastal Way (180 miles) not forgetting the Eden Source-to-Sea Walk (90 miles). The mixed woodland attracts flocks of siskin and redpoll, with Arctic redpoll once found upriver by the hospital. Jays have added acorns to the scrub and new oaks are popping up here and there. In the clearings both common spotted and early purple orchids grow alongside bird's foot trefoil, common twayblade, hedge bedstraw and crosswort. The real gem is an uncommon form of dune helleborine which loves old railway slag and may well be the rare Tyne helleborine.

The river here has several breeding birds, with dipper, grey and pied wagtail, redshank, oystercatcher and common sandpiper. The rough grassland on the opposite bank is used by hunting barn owl and little owl, kestrel and buzzard. Sparrowhawks can often be seen hunting on both sides of the river. A railway bridge crosses the river here from the old Carlisle to Edinburgh (Waverley) line. The hawthorn here also attracts fieldfare and redwing in winter, with the occasional waxwing. There is a big gull breeding colony downstream on Rockcliffe Marsh, with many of these gulls patrolling the river. Both herring and black-headed gull are found all year round, with lesser black-backed gull in summer and common gull in winter. Great black-backed gull can be found feeding on dead salmon in late autumn. Winter sees both woodcock and snipe feeding around the Lonning, along with goosander, cormorant and goldeneye on the river.

Otters love this section of the river and can be seen during daylight hours, especially in winter. Mink are not as common as they used to be and it has been suggested that the increasing otter population has helped to reduce their numbers. A new addition to the mammals here is polecat, once driven to extinction by shooting estates. Increasing numbers of rabbits have helped this reintroduction back onto the map and polecats can now be found right along the river.

The trail takes you through Bitts Park and Rickerby Park, again run by Carlisle City Council. Bitts Park is full of ornamental planting with sports areas, and the River Caldew adds its water to the Eden. Where these two rivers join stands Carlisle Castle, once the site of a Roman fort. The Roman name for Carlisle was Luguvalio. The castle was built by William II in 1093, and it changed hands several times during the Scottish wars, the most famous change of ownership coming during the 1745 uprising when it fell to Bonnie Prince Charlie.

Crossing over the Eden Bridge you enter Rickerby Park and will see on the left large numbers of meadow ant mounds. This species used to be very common on

27

uncultivated grassland but the effects of modern machinery, heavy stocking rates of cattle and sheep and the use of chemicals on the land have left this ant with few places to establish itself. The steep banking here has kept the mounds intact, making what must be a rare sight in a city nowadays.

The park itself has tall, scattered trees and cattle and sheep often graze the area. Some of the trees have hollow trunks, offering nest sites for jackdaw and stock dove. Birds along the river include kingfisher, grey wagtail, sedge warbler and goosander. The otters here are very tolerant of dog walkers and it is not uncommon to see them, even this close to the city centre. Grassland plants here include rest harrow, yarrow, bird's foot trefoil and huge quantities of celandine. This is a classic woodland plant but here the river has spread its seed across the grassland and the spring show is amazing.

Above the park was the Roman fort of Stanwix, its former presence now only hinted at by a small section of exposed stone in the car park of the Cumbria Park Hotel. Further north along the River Esk lies the scouting fort at Netherby (Castra Exploratorum) which was used to supply information on the many hostile tribes living to the north of the Wall. Again, as with Stanwix, there is not much to be seen as the private hall of the estate was built over the site, with many a stone in its walls taken from the original fort. The local village surrounding the fort has moved downstream to become Longtown.

The river here is part of the migration route for birds moving via the Solway and many rare birds have been blown this far into the Esk. The former gravel pits here at Longtown have become recreational sites for birdwatching and fishing and the sites boast a long list of bird species including ospreys, black terns, spotted and pectoral sandpiper (both from America), ferruginous duck and little gull. It is also one of the best places in Cumbria to see smew.

The Wall leaves the River Eden and moves out into agricultural land around Walby, often used by pink-footed geese and whooper swans in winter. A small flash in a field here (NY438596) has brought in both geese and swans to feed and bathe, as well as many waders on migration dropping in from the Tyne Gap. They have included ruff, dunlin, black-tailed godwit, greenshank and spotted redshank. The River Irthing, another tributary of the Eden, meanders around the flood plain, pushing the Wall onto higher ground to skirt the river at Irthington, Walton and Lanercost, home to a famous priory.

Most of this land was in the hands of the Scots until as late as 1157, with the priory founded in 1169. Again it was the Wall that suffered, with cut stone to build the priory ready for the taking and extra stone available from the many quarries left by the Romans. The name Lanercost is Gaelic for 'clearing in the wood' and today large areas of woodland are scattered across the higher ground at this point of the Irthing valley. Edward I visited the site both in 1280 and again, in ill health,

Lanercost Priory

in 1306. Robert the Bruce wrecked the place in 1311 but did nowhere near as much damage as Henry VIII, who dissolved the monasteries in 1538, after which all the lead was stripped from the priory roof.

The priory is now home to hundreds of bats which moved out of the old pub across the bridge. The pub had been their summer home but they moved to the priory for winter when the landlord blocked up the holes which they used to enter the building.

The old bridge here was built in 1724 and otters and goosander can often be seen at a deep pool alongside. Dippers nest on the bridge itself, and swallows and sand martins hunt insects over the water. The river and Wall run parallel to each other all the way up to Willowford where the old Roman bridge crossed the river. Brown trout are the most common fish found here and they enjoy the many caddis and stone fly that live in the river.

The Wall moves east, leaving the drainage from the area to run to the Solway. Far to the south is the South Tyne, dropping from Alston down to Hexham to join the North Tyne and where the Tyne itself starts. A wonderful car or bike journey takes you up a tributary of the Tyne to visit another Roman site.

The drive or bike ride starts just off the A69 with the turning for Ridley Hall and the Allen Banks National Trust site (NY796648). Start by crossing the river and keep on the minor road, turning right where it is signposted for Beltingham. Wind back to the river where you will find the Northumbrian Wildlife Trust reserve of Beltingham River Gravels (NY785640). This reserve has a Roman connection as the plants this reserve was made for are all indicators of heavy metal contamination. These heavy metals have drifted down the Tyne, especially from the mining of lead in its higher reaches. The Romans used the same lead on their houses and buildings around the country. Not only did they encourage this

29

mining, but they built a fort high up in the Pennines to protect their interests. The main heavy metals were thought to be brought down by the river from 1750 to 1960 when the Alston area was at the peak of its mining history.

This reserve boasts several interesting plants. It is one of only 21 sites in the world for the Tyne helleborine, a relative of the dune helleborine. Other indicators of the presence of lead include spring sandwort (whose other English name is leadwort). Alpine penny cress and mountain pansy have come down from the high moors to grow here but thrift, or sea pink, is nowhere near the sea here. So rare is this habitat that it has been given its own name: calaminarian grassland.

The grassland is just through the gate on your right but it is very small, so don't blink or you might miss it. The woodland here is where you find the helleborine but there are several birds here, including blackcap, long-tailed tit and even cuckoo. This narrow road comes to a turning spot at a footbridge across the Tyne to Bardon Mill. On the bridge are large patches of English stonecrop.

Only half a mile along this road is the famous Willimoteswick Castle, started in the twelfth century by the Ridleys, a family who are still in the area today. The most famous of them was Bishop Nicholas Ridley, burnt at the stake by Queen Mary in 1555. This building is more of a bastle than a castle but very impressive. Large numbers of swallows and house martins use the farm buildings around the castle.

Willimoteswick Castle

This is a dead-end road so return to the junction by Ridley Hall and head past the entrance of Allen Banks and follow the twisty road around the woodland onto the A686 towards Alston. The road drops steeply down to the River Allen, with more views across the rich woodland, and then rises up onto the moors before Alston. Look out for both red and black grouse with the occasional short-eared owl. On reaching Alston, carry on along this road until you hit the A689 signposted for Brampton.

Only a mile out of the town you reach the Gilderdale Valley, with parking just over the bridge (NY702485). There is a stile to take you into the field. A gentle walk upstream gives you potential views of several birds. In the plantation opposite the walk you can see or hear redstart, nuthatch, tree creeper, blackcap and willow warbler. The open fields here have meadow pipit, skylark, lapwing, curlew and redshank. The Gilderdale Beck has both dipper and grey wagtail breeding on it, while common sandpiper, nesting back off the water, enjoy the insect larvae along its banks. Look out for ring ouzel and tree pipit along the valley.

You reach a footbridge (NY698479) over the water where the Pennine Way long-distance trail drops down. Follow this trail back up the valley side and onto lambing fields to reach a high Roman fort called Whitley Castle (NY695488). There is open access to the area but do not climb the many modern stone walls found around the fort. The fort is now covered by turf with no stones showing but the ramparts are described as unique: no other fort in the Roman Empire had such elaborate defences.

The flora here is limited due to sheep grazing but the views around the area take some beating, especially if the skylark is singing above you on your visit. You can view the South Tyne valley which you will follow downstream. Walk back the way you came or follow the tracks back to the main road and back to your car. The walk is around two miles (three kilometres) long. Carry on along the A689 and pass another Northumberland Wildlife Reserve at Williamston (NY681521) on your right, just before the village of Slaggyford. This is also a calaminarian grassland, with birch scrub and gorse being managed to prevent the area from returning to woodland.

Another mile on from here, look out for Knarsdale (NY678539) where you drop off the main road to cross the South Tyne at Eals, and follow the road high up overlooking the river until you see the spectacular Lambley viaduct (NY676586). This was built in 1852 as part of the Alston railway, joining the main Carlisle to Newcastle line to carry lead and coal. The viaduct is 800 feet long, the centre spans are 110 feet high and the bridge is 11 feet wide.

It now has access from the minor road from Coanwood. There is a car park at NY679596, turning left in the village. The walk or bike ride will take you onto the viaduct to enjoy more amazing views upriver back towards Eals and downriver towards Featherstone Castle. This has been a great place to watch out for birds of prey over the years, with species like peregrine falcon, hobby, osprey, goshawk, rough-legged buzzard and honey buzzard all having been seen from here.

You can now drop back to the A69 to complete your circular route either via Featherstone Castle (NY674610) – which had its own prisoner of war camp for officers during World War Two – and Park Village, or on towards Plenmeller Common (see the Heather moorland chapter). Here you pass Coanwood Pond, created from subsidence after coal workings in the area. This pond had one famous bittern which was shot by a shooting party consisting of a lord and an earl. 'It flew like a hen harrier so we shot it,' was their plea. Both birds are supposed to be protected by law.

The total circular drive or bike ride is roughly 40 miles. We will rejoin the River Tyne later on its journey to the North Sea.

Last sighting –
stiff tail as
adult dived

Late evening, swimming

Diving

Adult Otter swimming, June

Otter

Silvanus, god of the forest

An altar to the god of the forest, engraved with the words 'Deo Silv', was found at Netherby, site of the scouting fort. It is hard to understand how much of the forest was still intact but what we call ancient woodland is often found on steep valley sides from which the axeman could not easily remove timber and where the land was no use for cultivation unless it had been terraced.

The woodland at Lower Gelt (NY520593) is a good example, with steep slopes running down to the River Gelt. Upstream the Middle Gelt woodland (NY532573) was less fortunate, with a clear fell of ancient oak woodland having been replanted with conifers. I managed these two woods for a time and in Middle Gelt the natural regeneration and coppice growth of oak was managed to allow the oak to come up along with the conifers. Sadly, when I left, the future management of the woods meant that many trees were lost as the conifers were allowed to dominate and kill off the oak.

The oak in Lower Gelt are growing on red sandstone which

Ancient woodland

can be seen in the river bed, giving an acid flora with many areas dominated by bilberry, woodrush and ferns. Wood sage, wood sorrel and wood anemone are limited but extensive beech regeneration is starting to dominate the oak and shade out the ground vegetation.

The birdlife here can be special, particularly in the spring and summer, with pied flycatcher, redstart and wood warbler. Adding to the birds on the Gelt are dipper and grey wagtail. The sandstone in the river has created several narrow gorges and on one bend several potholes have been dug out of the sandstone by harder boulders. This is also a great place to watch salmon and sea trout migrating upriver to spawn in the autumn. You can sit peacefully, away from the main path, and allow your mind to concentrate on this narrow piece of water through which the fish have to pass.

The Written Rock of Gelt is a Roman inscription made by the soldiers working the quarry here. It is found next to the river on the only cliff in this section of the wood and is hard to see. It is quite dangerous to climb the sandstone steps dug into the cliff face. Other inscriptions have been found in Middle Gelt which you can walk to just off the public path.

Middle Gelt has its charms as well, with one large cliff face where kestrels often nest, high up. Amongst the remaining oak you can find Douglas fir, Norway spruce, hybrid larch and western hemlock. Birch has regenerated with the oak and much of it remains. Footpaths take you through both woods, while at the entrance to Middle Gelt you find a skewwhiff viaduct (NY532573) taking the Carlisle to Newcastle railway over the Gelt.

The house here used to be a pub and the story goes that the architect carved the angle of the viaduct on a turnip to make sure that it was built correctly, with all the stones having to be cut at an angle to fit the model. The Gelt is blessed by more woodland at Talkinhead with one area of hanging oak woodland followed by another clear fell with conifers on the higher ground and broadleaved woodland below. This woodland has traces of limestone so plants are very good, with herb Paris, marjoram, lily of the valley, bird's nest and early purple orchid, guilder rose and sword-leaved helleborine.

The Upper Gelt has ancient woodland of its own, not on steep slopes but adapted to grazing pressure, with the northern limit of field maple in England as well as trees growing inside trees, creating some bizarre shapes and sizes. Here the main species are alder, ash, birch and hazel. Toothwort, a parasitic plant, grows in the old hazel roots while crab apple is quite common here in comparison with most woods.

The area around Brampton was left with glacial deposits called drumlins, many of which have trees planted on them. In this area beech was the favoured tree, often with hedges creating very close growth. Talkin Tarn, a country park

34

(NY543584), has this beech edge along with mixed planting inside. The glacier also dug out the tarn which is very unusual, as no water flows directly into it but a small stream drains out of it. It is fed by underwater springs. Wildlife here is very mixed, with winter wildfowl and summer migrants, while flora includes the sword-leaved helleborine and northern bilberry. Red squirrels come to the feeders here.

Crossing the divide towards the Irthing Valley is Milton Rigg Wood (NY559612) owned by the Woodland Trust. This is not ancient valley woodland but a long-term commercial oak woodland now owned by the Trust. A stone circle was once found here suggesting that it was open ground thousands of years ago, and the presence of Naworth Castle just yards down towards the Irthing again suggests that there were no trees here in the thirteenth century.

Naworth Castle

Plants here include bird's nest orchid, broad-leaved and green-flowered helleborine (the most northerly record for this plant), common wintergreen and common cow wheat. A new pond and boardwalk allow you to get close to the dragonflies with common and southern hawker, four-spot chaser and several damselflies. Naworth Castle now has its own private woods but dropping to the river is Quarry Beck (NY551627). A small area of oak and beech gives way to a conifer plantation. Otters use the beck and drop down to the big pool on the Irthing by Lanercost Bridge.

On the line of the Hadrian's Wall footpath is Comb Crag. The top of the wood may not look too exciting, with mixed Norway spruce and beech on one side and birch scrub on the other, but as the gradient drops back to the River Irthing you find a mature stand of Scots pine, sessile oak, ash and sycamore. The floor is covered in wild garlic, lesser celandine, ferns and woodrush but the path around the wood is often quite spectacular. Special plants include globe flower, northern bedstraw, early purple and bird's nest orchid. A sheet of red sandstone holds several acid-loving plants including juniper, cowberry, bilberry, bell heather and common heather. The cowberry is normally found high up on the fells and is very rare at this height.

The ridge here has many large Scots pine trees but it is the view into the canopy of other trees growing below that makes this site special. Look out for red squirrels, redstarts and pied flycatchers in summer, with jays and crossbills in winter. Walking upstream there is one section of western hemlock and a lovely humpbacked bridge. The stream under the bridge has a solid whin sill floor with its patterned stone work where water has eroded the stone. Morel, a very good eating mushroom, was once found here on the woodland floor. Crossing the bridge is a section of hanging oak woodland which is now very rare in the area.

Another remarkable area of woodland is found at Gilsland Gorge (NY634687). Once dominated by broadleaved woodland, many conifers – larch, Douglas fir, Norway spruce and Scots pine – now add to the landscape's colours. Sitka spruce plantations dominate the area as part of the Spadeadam Forest so these broad-leaved trees seem out of place to the modern eye. The area is famous for its spa

fed by sulphur springs and the 'popping stone' once visited by Sir Walter Scott, where he is thought to have 'popped the question' to his future wife. The stone was a famous visitor attraction as it was thought to be a fertility symbol, its shape suggesting a sexual act.

To find more accessible broadleaved woodland you have to cross over to the South Tyne. Here is an area of woodland as large as any previously mentioned, running up the River Allen, a tributary of the Tyne. There are several owners, with the National Trust in charge of Allen Banks and Staward Gorge, the Northumberland Wildlife Trust owning Briarwood Banks and the Forestry Commission involved with most of the rest. There are several walks through the area, with a six-mile walk up to Cupola Bridge where the A686 Haydon Bridge to Alston road cuts the River Allen.

Parts of this woodland, especially the Briarwood section, are described as the best in Northumbria. Although some form of forestry activity has taken place elsewhere, many of the broadleaved trees are spectacular. Add to that the size of the River Allen and its many gorges and cliff faces and you have the makings of a wonderful walk. Several bridges allow you to change sides. Some paths are suitable for wheelchairs and pushchairs but the scramble along the undulating paths will tire the kids.

As an ancient woodland site, the flora has its indicators like wild garlic, woodruff, enchanter's nightshade, dog's mercury and some bluebells. Ferns abound in the damp conditions with male and ladies' fern, broad buckler and the rarer beech fern. Wood fescue is a rare grass found here, along with some of the species previously mentioned in other woods, like bird's nest orchid, herb Paris and toothwort.

There is an area of heavy metal contamination in some of the river grasslands with mountain pansy growing well downstream of its normal upland area. At present, the woodlands are classified as the most northern distribution of dormouse. The Romans brought its big cousin, the edible dormouse, to Britain and its remains have been found well to the south, but this little creature has survived deforestation around the area to hang on in these valleys. It is a very secretive animal, coming out only at night, and the use of bird nest boxes may throw light on the true number found in the area.

Another mammal just hanging on is the red squirrel, with broadleaved woodland being the best habitat for its rival, the introduced grey squirrel. Trapping takes place to try to reduce the grey which carries a disease which can wipe out the reds. No work has yet been done on the predators that prefer the grey as prey, such as the goshawk and pine marten, which themselves have been wiped out by game estates in many areas of Britain.

As in the woodlands of Cumbria, the big three migrants – the pied flycatcher, redstart and wood warbler – are found in these woods. This is the highest density of pied flycatchers in Northumbria and nest boxes are provided in some areas to boost the population. The cliffs here once held the peregrine falcon which enjoyed feeding on the many woodland birds. Buzzards are now common, having suffered the same fate as the goshawk in the past. Rare falcons like hobby and merlin use the airspace, while the rare honey buzzard is the dream bird of any Tyneside birder standing on the Cupola Bridge, which offers great open views of the surrounding steep-sided woodland.

These woodlands also offer the opportunity to find all three British wood-peckers. The great spotted woodpecker has expanded greatly in recent years, its numbers up by 20%. The opposite is true of the smaller, lesser spotted wood-pecker which in some recent years was not even recorded in Northumbria. This woodland would seem to have great potential for this bird, though, and in winter it is worth checking the roving tit flocks to find it. Green woodpecker is more of a ground feeder but several pairs are found in the valley.

Great spotted woodpecker

Heather moorland

In Roman times, heather moorland was not a common habitat in this area. It came to the fore in Victorian times with the rise in popularity of red grouse shooting. In some areas there is an increase of birdlife on these moors but in many more, birds and mammals are destroyed by people who call them vermin and who want to try to keep high numbers of red grouse.

One of the best areas to observe wildlife is around Plenmeller (NY7461). The area is criss-crossed with roads and you can enjoy views of birds and mammals from the comfort of your car. Some of the area was used for open-cast mining between 1991 and 2000, during which time 1.91 million tons of coal were removed. The area is now a mixture of grassland, heather moor and wet flushes.

Some of the star birds here include merlin, short-eared owl and hen harrier. All three depend on a good supply of smaller species. The merlin feeds on meadow pipit, skylark and, in particular, the starlings which use the grassland, while the owl and the harrier love the abundance of voles. Another benefit to the hen harrier is that the area is overrun with rabbits, so ringtails (females) in particular use the area in winter. These rabbits also encourage many buzzards, goshawks and even rough-legged buzzards to use the area.

The other special bird here is the black grouse which in the spring can be seen lekking (displaying) from the road. Numbers have varied in recent years due to bad winters and a lack of trees for them to feed on, but there are always some around, their numbers often boosted by birds moving away from Geltsdale. I have watched up to ten cocks displaying from the road junction with the Whitfield road (NY739589). Grey hens (females) have perched on roadside fences and cocks often fly across the road.

Golden plover can often be seen in springtime from this same point, before nesting higher up the fells. Large numbers concentrate on the farmland, often in their hundreds, but as many as 1,500 have been counted. This attracts hunting peregrine falcons to the area. They were once a common breeding bird of the area but have now been removed from red grouse moors. Other waders here include lapwing, a common breeding bird, along with redshank, snipe, oystercatcher and curlew.

Wet hollows with plenty of water attract black-headed gulls to nest here. They help to protect other birds nesting around their colonies: wigeon, teal and mallard will only breed where these gulls are found. Joining these gulls has been the rarer Mediterranean gull. Other rarities found in the area include wintering snow buntings which are normally found much higher up on the Pennines.

In recent years large numbers of what some call feral geese have joined the crowds of other birds enjoying the area. Canada geese, originally brought over as a present to James I, are now breeding in the area, with a winter population of sometimes more than 100 birds. One of the main reasons for an increase in this population is the removal of all ground predators, allowing the geese plenty of protection.

The roads also have their fair share of smaller birds, with meadow pipit, skylark and wheatear being the most common. Red grouse often sit on roadside walls, especially when holding territory, using the height to warn off other cocks from their ground.

The rabbits become carrion on the road as cars hit them at night, bringing down crows and even gulls to feed on them. Sadly a red kite was poisoned here, having fed on a poisoned carcass. Poison is a common way of reducing the crow population, even though to use it is to break the law.

Other moorland worth a visit includes Geltsdale, and an area along the A686 between Alston and Haydon Bridge. Also the minor road from Allendale to Nenthead, and Hexhamshire Common from the B6295.

Short-eared owl

Birdoswald and up the Irthing

The name Birdoswald may suggest a connection with birds, but how the name evolved from the Roman name Banna, meaning 'spur of land', is a mystery. It seems to derive from the Anglo-Saxon and was probably the name of the farmer who worked the land here. The location of this fort would have made escape from attack an unlikely option, as a meander in the River Irthing cuts the fort off from the south.

As a result, another fort was built at Bewcastle, seven miles to the north, to warn this garrison if an attack was coming. The meanders in the river offer the visitor amazing views, the best outlook being from behind the fort (NY615662), where a steep area of woodland and rolling farmland stand out, looking back into the High Pennines of Cold Fell and the RSPB reserve at Geltsdale.

The site was once owned by Lord Henley of Scaleby Castle, who happened to build his castle with Roman stone. The mixed habitats here offer a wide range of species, with a nice five-kilometre circular walk to see more of the Wall and its surrounding area.

A visitor centre here doubles as a home for wildlife, with several pairs of swallows using the buildings to build their nests. A camera relays the activity to the tearoom so that visitors do not miss out. More secretive are the bats: so far, pipistrelle and whiskered have been found here, using the buildings as nurseries and hibernation sites.

The viewpoint can offer your first encounter with roe deer as they graze below, and the updraught of the steep valley draws birds of prey to glide around the area. Here you might see buzzard, goshawk, kestrel and sparrowhawk, while the passage of gulls using the Tyne Gap sees hundreds or even thousands of common gulls arriving from Europe in the autumn.

The woodland here is too steep to venture down and the flora has little contact with the public. Globe flower is a great species still found growing along the river, along with early purple orchid, twayblade, common spotted orchid, toothwort and lady's smock, the food plant of the orange-tip butterfly.

New planting of broadleaved trees has helped to hold the banking together but down at the ruined farm the meander is trying to cut through the bank to reach the other side. Here its river cliff is home to a large colony of sand martins which attract the rare hobby to hunt them for food. One of Cumbria's first nesting records for this species was found close to this sand martin colony.

The river has breeding common sandpipers and oystercatchers, while both redshank and lapwing have faded away. Barn owls hunt on both sides of the river but the old Roman bridge disappeared years ago. The remains can be seen at Willowford where surrounding woodland holds marsh tit, wood warbler and pied flycatcher. Badgers are common around this land and it is possible to watch them at a sett to the left of the new suspension bridge.

The trail takes you into Gilsland so watch the river for sightings of dipper, grey and pied wagtail and goosander. Otters are now common in the area. You need to go left to cross the river again and then left again to walk along the road back to Birdoswald. There are great views back into the valley, with possible sightings of redstarts and woodpeckers. Before long, you go left again and look down onto Midgeholme Moss.

This area of land has been drained to increase grazing but, under high level stewardship, water is being put back on the bog to encourage both plants and birds to use the site once more. At present, large areas of cotton grass demonstrate its wet history, but species like sphagnum mosses and cranberry are expected to increase, helping species like black grouse to come back into the area. Winter records of hen harrier, merlin and goshawk have already shown that the area is supporting a mixture of bird species.

The wader population of the early 1980s has declined due to this draining and species like lapwing, curlew, redshank and snipe should improve in numbers. Yellow flag is growing in the lower reaches of the moss, along with many sedges, like lesser pond sedge. These provide seed for reed bunting that already breed here. From here you can see the car park for Birdoswald and it is time to try another great site in the area.

Bewcastle (NY565746), only seven miles away, is well worth a visit. Of the fort, only the ramparts remain, but a church has been built on the site, home to a cross dedicated to King Alefrid who ruled around 670 A.D. It is the best example in Europe of a cross from this period. Clearly visible on the four-sided cross is the image of a raven, a bird highly valued as a pet by the Romans but sacred to the seafaring Anglo-Saxons who came after them.

The area is wild, like the area up the Irthing, scattered with isolated farms and dominated by forestry, with an area of moorland separating the Kershope from the Spadeadam forest. As late as 2010, a new-to-science species of fern was found high on the gritstone outcrops, a hybrid between Wilson's filmy fern and Tunbridge filmy fern and yet to be named.

Returning to the Irthing gorge (NY634687) there is a large hotel on top of the gorge where you can park. A sulphur spring runs through the gorge itself, creating the location for the hotel and the Popping Stone. Past the hotel is a road leading to Moscow, in reality the name of a farm but also the location in the 1950s and 1960s for one of Britain's

Bewcastle Cross

contributions to the space race, with the famous Blue Streak rocket being tested here. The area is still a military base but today is one of Europe's main radar stations for training pilots.

Turning right for Churnsike (NY625688) you will see that large areas of Forestry Commission plantation have been felled to make way for mock tanks, aircraft and buildings. Some of the clear felling here is to improve the land for black grouse. A variety of bird species can be found here, including raven, peregrine falcon, kestrel and nightjar. Botanically the Irthing Gorge extends up to Crammel Linn waterfall and offers a home to alpine plants like yellow mountain saxifrage and alpine bistort.

To follow this narrow road is a great way to get the feel of such an isolated part of Britain. Grassland stretches for miles, with green belts of forestry creeping in as you pass Horseholme Farm. Roe deer can be seen here and, in late June, small pearl-bordered fritillary butterflies feed on the marsh thistles. In good cone years, flocks of both crossbill and siskin are common in the conifers. You are soon out of the enclosed forest and looking across the meandering Irthing valley with the Natural England reserve of Gowk Bank (NY680735) on your right. This may look like many other areas of grassland and scrub but it holds a wide variety of plants due to an outcrop of lime in this acid wilderness.

Orchids are one of the highlights of this site, leading to a large number of studies on the hybrids in particular: northern marsh crossing with common spotted, heath spotted crossing with northern marsh and so on. Fortunately there are plenty of pure orchids to look at, with fragrant, frog and small white being some of the best. Species like yellow rattle and eyebright help to keep the grass from dominating, as they both feed on the grass's roots. Banks of melancholy thistle and globe flower add to the wood cranesbill and meadowsweet.

Willow scrub is an impossible challenge for the plants so some management is needed to keep the willow in check. Birds here include redpoll, willow warbler and reed bunting and, by the river, common sandpiper and sedge warbler.

The road now takes you via Butterburn Farm onto Butterburn Flow (NY670750). This is the largest of the 58 border mires (blanket bogs) covering 1,200 acres of Cumbria and Northumbria and is unique in obtaining moisture from groundwater rather than simply from rainfall. It is intact, given that so much forestry has been created around its edge, but this closing in has reduced the number of bird species using the area today. This was a former lekking area for black grouse, but that is now nothing more than a memory. It is hoped that good management will bring this species back to the area and possibly, one day, to this lek.

Other species, like golden plover and dunlin, were widespread before the planting of trees, and a survey on Bewcastle Fells, which rises above this forest, found only two pairs of golden plover. Curlew are also very restricted, with skylark and meadow pipit making up the bulk of the bird species using the flow. Hunting merlin, hen harrier and goshawk do venture over the flow and buzzards are a new species now nesting around its edge.

45

It is the flora, though, which makes the site work, with sphagnum species holding the water while sedges and rushes enjoy it at their feet. Two rare sedges include few-flowered and bog sedge, while white beak-sedge is also here. Greater sundew is common and bog rosemary, creeping willow and deer grasses are also found. It is the isolation of this journey which makes it unique and although you have to return the same way, bikers and walkers can actually use the forest tracks and go all the way across to Kielder.

Returning to the main road, another historic site worth visiting is Thirlwall Castle. (Thirlwall, the family name, means 'hole in the wall'.) This is a pilgrimage for Yorkists, as Percival Thirlwall was the standard bearer at the Battle of Bosworth, where he was killed, along with 'Good' King Richard, as the Northumbrian Percys turned traitor and swapped sides in the battle. This ruined castle, built with Roman stone, is now a great site for bats and swifts. In some years, around ten pairs of swifts can be seen screaming their way around the remains and nesting in the old stone walls.

The bats can be of several species, with whiskered and Brandt's, pipistrelle and the large noctule using hollow trees to roost in the area. The castle walls hold a number of interesting lichen. A small area of meadow and woodland is also being managed here by the Northumberland National Park with a lease from Thirlwall Castle Farm. Species like greater burnet and betony show that the meadow is an historic one, while pignut is a classic plant of grassland. In the woodland is a stand of aspen, a rare tree in its natural state with only a few clumps found on the whin sill along the Wall.

Curlew

Geltsdale

The RSPB reserve at Geltsdale began its life way back in 1975, thanks to the discovery, by one of the owners, of a badger caught in a snare. As the family enjoyed wildlife, an agreement was reached between the society and the family. Tarnhouse Farm and the shooting rights had been obtained by the family from the Howards of Naworth Castle when the estate was broken up in 1962. This once grand estate being divided between several relations. The reserve originally covered three farms – Geltsdale, Tarnhouse, and Halton Lea Farm – and the shooting rights gave the owners total access.

Agriculture here dates back 4,000 years, when terraces were cut high up on the fells, 1,000 feet above sea level, to grow crops on the side of what is called Tarnmonath. By the time the Romans came to the area these uplands must have served as a food source, supplying natural game such as red deer, wild boar and black grouse.

The Normans introduced the idea of the King's Forest, in which hunting laws prevented peasants from stealing game. By 1500 A.D., more than a thousand red deer were recorded on the fells. This level of grazing would have reduced the number of trees growing in the area as well as the heather moorland which is found today. These deer would have been used to feed the many armies which travelled north and south from here during the Scottish wars. As well as the armies passing through, these border areas had their own feuds with the reivers, family clans which never saw the border as a barrier to thieving and pillaging over a wide area, often stealing cattle.

Surprisingly, it was not recorded when these red deer became extinct in this area of the Pennines; Macpherson's *Fauna of Lakeland 1892*, the bible for Cumbria's early natural history, talks only about the Lake District's herds, some of which still exist today. It is possible that it was around 1745, when the last Scots army came through these parts. Charles Stewart (Bonnie Prince Charlie) stayed at Brampton, as the castle at Carlisle gave in easily. Then came the English army, which would have stayed in the area long after the castle was retaken and the Scots army defeated at the Battle of Culloden.

Another historic feature of Geltsdale was the drovers' road (NY582540), thought to have been made in the Middle Ages. This was a wide, open road used to move cattle and sheep from the Scottish border down to Penrith and on towards London. Thousands of stock could be moved in this way and, because of the threat from reivers, even an encampment or village (NY571552) was made, well off the road and close to the River Gelt, to protect stock from attack. The movement of stock this way came to an end with the age of the train.

The landscape of Geltsdale was changed when coal was found in the area. First came bell pits, going straight down into the ground, followed by drift pits, cutting into the side of the Geltsdale fells. Mining brought hundreds of workers into the area and saw the construction of new communities and terraces of houses. The movement of coal created the early wagon ways, which led to some of the earliest railway systems in the world. These railways gave birth to the standard gauge, used around the world, of 1.435 mm (4 ft 8½ in.), so when travelling by train, give a thought to Lord Carlisle's railway and Geltsdale, where it all started.

These fells were home to so much industry that steam locomotives were made at Kirkhouse, Hallbankgate, close to the fells. Coal was also used to burn lime, so lime quarries and lime kilns were worked around Geltsdale, using the trains to transport the resulting fertiliser around the area.

At one time, the Gairs pit in the Gelt Valley employed 350 men, and there were many more mines in the area besides that one. Later in its life, in 1836, even the now famous Rocket, invented by George Stevenson in 1829, was bought by Lord Carlisle. The engine only worked until 1840, when it was considered too light to pull the expanding coal wagons. It was left to rust in the Kirkhouse works before being offered to the British Museum.

The invention of the gun brought a surge in the popularity of red grouse shooting, especially when Queen Victoria made it a royal occasion in Scotland. The Glorious Twelfth was in fact the day when Members of Parliament left London on holiday, heading north to pursue this so-called sport. The uplands were seen in those days as a plaything and were managed for heather, the main food of the red grouse.

Fire was a tool on the moor, preventing any trees from establishing themselves and creating an acid environment in which heather would grow. Strip burning gave the moors the look of a chequerboard, adding an age system to the heather. Young heather provided food for the red grouse and older heather became their nesting areas. Many birds and mammals were killed to protect the numbers of red grouse, their remains hung on a gibbet to show the master what a good job the gamekeeper was doing.

In the 1970s and 1980s the moor was drained to improve growing conditions for the heather. This was to have a major effect not just on the water catchment but also on the peat itself, causing heavy run-off and drying of the peat. This same drainage exacerbated the flooding of Carlisle in 2005, costing £500 million – a high price for a few red grouse.

Another big change came to Geltsdale in 1898 when the Carlisle Water Company started building the Castle Carrock reservoir, installing several miles of piping to run water from the springs in the Old Water and the New Water to help fill it. Even a railway was erected along the Gelt to bring the materials up to Binney Banks and beyond. The work was finished in 1905 and it was opened in 1909 by the Mayor of Carlisle. Damage to springs caused by draining for red grouse has caused the present-day water company to take supplies direct from the river, with another £1.7 million needed to clean sediment from this water.

Sheep farming has been the main agricultural feature for many years, with mainly Scottish black-faced sheep on both sides of the hill. Before fencing, goats were used to keep the sheep in their area of the fell but the last record of goats on Geltsdale was in around 1900. Wild goats are still found in the Bewcastle area, especially around Christianbury Crags. Sheep numbers increased dramatically from 1947 with the introduction of a direct payment per head.

When the RSPB came to Geltsdale they had access only onto what was then 12,000 acres of mainly heather moorland, but this also included Tindale Tarn, several small pockets of woodland, small rivers and streams and open grassland. The first warden, Dick Squires, was classed as a summer warden, which meant that he was on site from April to August but that no-one covered the winter period. His first task was to survey the area to see what wildlife was present.

With such a large area to cover and with no knowledge of the terrain, this was an amazing task for the first warden to take on. He was based in the north of the reserve, near Hallbankgate, from where he had to drive the six miles to the southern area and another four miles from there to the south-east boundary. His first job, then, was to find his feet, before even beginning to try to work out which species were present across the range of birds, mammals, flora, butterflies and other insects.

The first few summer wardens all worked for one season only until Bob Gomes covered both 1977 and 1978. A winter warden, Nick Dymond, was asked to carry out some management in the wood at Talkinhead in 1980–1981, but on his own it was a big challenge. The RSPB finally decided to have a full-time warden, which is how I came on the scene in March 1981.

I had been chosen for the job as I had got on well with a difficult Welsh farmer when I worked under Dick Squires at Ynis Hir. Here at Geltsdale I had three farmers and a gamekeeper to deal with, as well as the family who owned part of the area but who owned the shooting rights to – and who gave the society access to – all 12,000 acres. We also expanded the reserve by adding 260 acres of woodland for me to manage. Making contact with local naturalists and birdwatchers was a key part of learning about the area so I got involved with the local natural history societies and RSPB members' groups.

The special birds on the reserve were merlin, peregrine falcon, golden plover, dunlin and a failing population of black grouse. The early years saw a crash in the yellow wagtail population, thought to be due to a drought in the Sahal region of Africa. Their numbers fell from six pairs to none. This was also the time when changes in farming practice saw a move from hay to silage, meaning an earlier cutting of the grass just where the wagtails nested. Another population was affected by the drought in Africa as sand martins fell from 100 to none in the same year.

The 1980s were interesting times in the uplands as sheep numbers were rising at an alarming rate. This was due to a direct, or headage, payment for the number of sheep held on each farm, meaning that the uplands were being eaten out of vegetation, including heather. One area between the Old and New Water, which join to make the River Gelt, was allowed to be fenced. In no time at all, thanks to what is known as mob stocking, the heather was gone altogether. This was to be a new lambing field. Before the end of this payment regime, up to 7,000 sheep were grazing the 12,000 acres.

51

The effect on black grouse was the most dramatic. There had been fewer than ten birds when I started, and this fell in no time to none. Any birds left in the area were at the new forestry plantation of Denton Fell to the north of the reserve, where ten cocks were lekking (displaying), but these too would disappear as the trees closed in.

The presence of a full-time warden was to have a dramatic effect on the number of peregrine falcons using the area. This bird was certainly enjoying a major recovery in Britain after the dark days of chemicals like DDT, but I had made the effort to approach every gamekeeper in the area and was always accepted into their houses. The single pair found at an old whin sill quarry was not producing many young, due to theft, but the surrounding area did have more adults moving in. A valley of the Gelt was soon to have the second pair on the reserve while a neighbouring shoot also had a pair. Next door, another shoot had two pairs and, further afield, even more pairs started to appear.

Many of the breeding ledges were expanded or constructed by me after advice from Geoff Horne, the main monitor of peregrines in Cumbria. In 1992, after I had left the RSPB, I even had a pair nest by my house. Two young were reared which became numbers 999 and 1,000 on the list of peregrines ringed by Geoff. Nearly all these pairs, including the pair by my house, disappeared in the late 1990s. My female was found shot.

I was a fit lad in those days and often cycled around the reserve, well before the era of mountain bikes. Botany was not my strong point but with the help of people like Jeremy Roberts, who found the new species of fern for the world on the Bewcastle Fells, the list grew beyond 680 species, indicating the variety of habitats held on the reserve. Ten species of orchid were found, including both common and lesser twayblade, frog orchid and the rare sword-leaved helleborine. Both adder's tongue and moonwort, small grassland ferns, were found, together along with sedges, grasses and more ferns.

The two ancient woodland areas of Knotts ('nuts') and Binney Banks were amazing in terms of tree growth. Trees like rowan and birch would often start growing on top of the old alder trees, their roots growing down inside the rotting alder until they reached the ground. As the new trees grew bigger, the wind would rock them until the old trunk of the alder would burst open, allowing the new trees to fall to the ground. They would then grow upwards again, leaving an amazing tangle of roots to be part of their trunk. Wild crab apple was common in these two woods, while there is only one field maple, here at its northern limit in Britain.

52

Another area which is often completely missed is the lane running up to the Greens, where two walls prevent grazing from the fell. Here the natural regeneration of many trees and shrubs has occurred. It is interesting to consider how the species arrived here in the first place, as this lane demonstrates how many tree species can find their way onto the fell once grazing is reduced.

Higher areas have birch, a tree with a seed which can be carried by the wind. As the wind hits the Wall the seed falls to the ground and takes root. Hawthorn has a seed which is carried in birds' stomachs after they have eaten the ripened fruit. In this case, the birds – black grouse or redwings – have left their droppings by the Wall, allowing the seeds within to germinate and grow. The rowan here could have been carried in the droppings of fieldfares, as they often roost on the open moor having eaten the fruit. There is one oak tree up the lane and it is likely to have grown from an acorn buried and never reclaimed by a jay, the only species known to travel great distances to store food for the winter. No mammal would have travelled as far as the lane from the parent tree way down in Hynam Wood. The single sycamore may well have been whipped up by a storm, as the famous 'helicopter' seed usually only moves a short distance from the parent tree to start a new life. A cherry is the newest species here, having probably been brought here by a blackbird which had eaten the many fruit in the newly-planted wood at Hynam. Cherries have the potential to spread by root growth (suckers) but in this case the tree is 100 yards from the nearest tree.

Around 190 species of bird have been recorded around the reserve, and Tindale Tarn was a great location to add breeding and passage bird species to the reserve list. During the days of mining, the glacial lake had been drained of at least 8–10 feet of water, to try and prevent water from entering the mines. This had left very shallow water with maximum depths of 10 feet, and only 4 feet in most areas. The then Earl of Carlisle had offered the public the chance to use either Tindale or Talkin Tarn for boating and, fortunately, they chose Talkin, leaving the tranquil waters of Tindale Tarn for wildlife.

There were no islands on the water and all four sides had originally been grazed. Suddenly future management here became a possibility, though, after two of the family's tenant farmers agreed to give up land for planting. This extra workload, along with the 260 acres of extended woodland, meant that new staff were needed. Twenty four temporary staff were taken on under a Job Creation scheme which lasted two years.

In 1983, through this verbal agreement, fencing was erected on the west and south sides of the tarn with small extended planting to the north on Tarnhouse Rigg and the southern flanks of Tindale Fell. Three islands were also placed at the west and east ends of the tarn, made up of stone collected from the north shore and pushed out by boat, showing how shallow the tarn was. This allowed black-headed gulls to nest for the first time on the reserve. Their presence helped other nesting birds, especially coot, which often lost their eggs to the bigger lesser black-backed gulls nesting at that time on Whitfield Lough, only a few miles to the east. Also on Whitfield were black-headed gulls which protected a special duck, the wigeon, another new bird to nest on the reserve and which soon came to Tindale to breed.

Many birds on passage came via the tarn, including one flock of 120 kittiwakes making their journey through the Tyne Gap. Barnacle geese were annual visitors, as were pink-footed geese, whooper swans, large numbers of duck including sea duck like common scoter, scaup and long-tailed duck, waders like greenshank, spotted redshank and green sandpiper, black tern and little gull. A great rarity, a little bittern, was found dead.

One of the most memorable birds was an avocet, seen feeding at the eastern end of the tarn at a time when it was very rare this far north. It is the emblem of the RSPB and turned up at a time when the BBC was making its first live broadcast from Minsmere, the *Radio Times* marking the occasion with an avocet on its front cover.

Bats now needed to be looked at under licence and I often used the expert advice of Pete Holden, then a ranger in the Northumberland National Park, his wife Liz and the Cumberland Bat Group. Bat boxes were erected in several woods and natural sites were located. One very interesting beech tree in Lower Gelt

Woods held noctule bats, their site a former set of woodpecker holes used first by starlings and then taken over by the bats.

Another bat site was discovered when a local pub landlord became upset about droppings falling into the restaurant below. Pete and I were asked to come – we thought – to monitor the roost. The site was between our wood at Quarry Beck and Boothby Bank, but also close to Lanercost Priory where we thought this group of bats wintered. We were allowed to stand on a flat roof as dusk approached and the landlord passed us up several pints of beer to keep us going. We thought this was very nice until, after we had counted 279 female pipistrelle bats leaving the roost, the landlord returned and asked if we had caught them all yet. We told him that we would need another licence to do that, given that they were a protected species, and gathered that we had been lucky to get the beer.

The work of a warden was not just on the reserve but extended to the local area, talking with schools, Women's Institutes and wildlife clubs. I even talked to landowners, farmers and gamekeepers well away from the reserve and its boundaries. There was many a tale to tell.

I had to deal with land agents and one day was asked to a meeting to discuss open-cast mining near Tindale village. An area of around 300 acres of land was earmarked for open cast by a mine operator who was so keen to get my, and the agent's, agreement to the scheme that he said that he would make it worth our while to agree with him. I burst out laughing. Didn't he know that I came from Yorkshire and that we do not do that sort of thing? Amazingly, not even the owners of the land knew what was happening as the agents had not told them. I phoned and let them know and the whole scheme was immediately dropped. What a way to run the land!

I also remember when a merlin was shot. I had already found the nest but on the day in question could not get the female to fly. Female merlins, nesting on the ground, are well known for sitting tight in thick heather. All too often the bird is seen returning to the nest but it is often hopeless trying to locate it, the thick heather offering no landmarks to use as guides.

In this case I did find her but she was dead, sitting on her clutch of four eggs. I picked her up and saw that she was carrying shot. She had flown back to the nest to die. I was furious as all my birds of prey were having a great time, expanding not just on the reserve area but on the adjoining moors. I summoned the two local keepers to one of their houses and put it to them that, either one of them had shot the bird, or that there were poachers operating on their moor. Nothing could be proven but at least they knew I knew, and the rest of the season was free of persecution.

A lot of time was also spent on a nest box scheme in the woodland, especially during the breeding season. Nest boxes were made by volunteers and donated by RSPB members' groups from as far away as Durham. In all, around 150 were erected, mostly in the hope of attracting the pied flycatcher. In all we had six pairs, mainly in Knotts Wood and Binney Banks. Nest boxes were erected in woods away from these two as the age of the trees there meant that there were plenty of holes for the birds to use.

In no time at all, pied flycatcher numbers rose to 98 pairs. This included an increase in Binney Banks and Knotts Wood, even though boxes had not been added there. Many other species benefited, especially the tit family and redstarts, who preferred bigger holes in the boxes where a great spotted woodpecker had opened them up. Even a great tit nibbling at the sides would make the hole wide enough for them.

Many of the woods needed management, including repairing fences, brashing well-established trees and weeding young trees. Footpaths had to be repaired, ponds built and trees thinned. A gang of 24 were kept busy and most of them enjoyed the work. One of the lads was an expert stone waller and, with many walls needing repair, we all learnt a lot from him.

We had a tractor and trailer to supply the extra stone, all of it coming from abandoned walls elsewhere. Fencing materials were delivered to the sites where needed, with many of the fence posts coming from a wood cleared of sitka spruce, and any spare firewood was delivered to the warden's house. A motorbike became my standard form of transport to get me to many of the isolated areas, while the teams enjoyed the back of the tractor and trailer.

Sadly, the good times were not to last. One bird which is now virtually extinct as a breeding bird in England was starting to turn up on the reserve. The hen harrier was occasionally seen, especially in autumn, with one male displaying in the Old Water one summer, probably having come from a failed nest. In 1988 a pair of fieldfares, yet another rare breeding bird in the UK, were using a valley not far from my house. This meant I spent more time up the valley and noticed a nesting pair of hen harriers on adjoining land. A pair raised four young that year.

In 1989 we had two pairs, one close to the previous year's nest and a new pair in the northern part of the reserve. Both nests were holding large young when they were attacked. Six young and a female were killed at one nest and four young and a male died at the other. A single chick was left there, with the female feeding it. A court case for disturbance was lost as the police refused to allow me to give evidence. As two of the three magistrates were linked to shooting, I think of it as having lost 2–1.

Volunteers watching this nest during the day had noticed a man running through the heather dragging something behind him. When they then saw dogs, the volunteers thought this was going to be an attack on the harrier chicks, but I told them about the Cumbrian tradition of hound trailing and they understood what they had been seeing. The man was pulling an aniseed-scented rag which the hounds would then follow. And by chance he had happened to enter the valley where the harriers were nesting.

Back to the killings. The owners of the land took the side of the shooting syndicate and they soon forgot all the good work I had done for them on the reserve. In 1990 I was moved away from the reserve to Staffordshire, only to return, having left the RSPB, in 1991. A short-term warden was brought in until Malcolm Stott, who had been my manager, took over. Even at this stage the RSPB could have walked away from the reserve but one of the farms came up for sale. This was Halton Lea Farm, just in Northumberland. Instead of buying the whole farm they bought the 1,000-acre fell in 1990.

Across the Scottish border, the first of the Langholm projects was getting started, which was to see hen harriers in Britain protected for the first time. The population went from a single pair to 24, meaning that this was also becoming a common bird at Geltsdale as the two areas are only 24 miles apart as the harrier flies. One pair raised five young in 1990 and by 1992, four pairs were nesting on or close to the boundaries, with other individuals around as well. Sadly, this population soon started to decline.

One incident captured on camera was of a female hen harrier being shot as RSPB staff and police watched from across the boundary. This was to become known as the 'balaclava killing' as the person responsible hid his face so as not to be recognised. The policeman present thought they had enough evidence, having witnessed the shooting, and did not cross the boundary to apprehend him. How, though, do you pick out one of eight men in a police identity parade when they are all wearing balaclava helmets?

Another big change in the reserve was that publicity was greatly reduced. RSPB members were not encouraged to visit. In my time we had RSPB members groups arriving in 52-seater buses from as far away as Birmingham, Leeds, Bradford and Manchester as well as Glasgow and Edinburgh. I went to give them talks in winter about the reserve and then gave them an escorted tour of the reserve in summer. The fact that there were fewer visitors meant that it was easier for birds of prey to disappear.

A small 70-acre field in the Gelt Valley was bought in 1998 for black grouse, the money coming from a national bird race. Another purchase was made in 1999 when the shooting rights were bought from the family, allowing the RSPB to manage the moor but not the grazing. The shooting press was furious that an historic shooting moor was no longer going to ring to the sound of guns on the Glorious Twelfth, the start in August of the red grouse shooting season.

In 2001 the area was hit by foot and mouth disease. Most of the sheep were killed and removed, leaving the farmer at Tarnhouse Farm with no stock. He took the opportunity to retire and this gave the society the chance of a real purchase: in 2002, they managed to buy the majority of the farm owned by the family. Again, as at Halton Lea, they did not buy the farmhouse and its surrounding fields. The society could now manage 5,500 acres in total, along with the Halton Lea land.

It was decided to bring in a tenant farmer who would manage the land in the way the RSPB wanted. The whole farm would go organic and cattle would be the major management tool, as their grazing helps to break up the ground and allow new plant material to germinate. Sheep numbers were reduced from 2,000 to 350. One of the drawbacks for potential candidates was that the society was only offering a small cottage rather than the normal type of farmer's accommodation. Interest came from farmers from as far away as St. Bees in West Cumbria and Hexham in Northumberland, as well as from local farmers, and finally a farmer who had worked with the National Trust was given the tenancy.

The RSPB also took over the tenancy of Clowsgill Farm as the farmer here retired. This covered the north shore of Tindale Tarn and stretched out onto Tarnhouse Fell, along with hay fields and Coalfell Beck. Again the farmhouse and buildings remained in the family and were rented out separately.

Back on the moor, hen harriers became scarce after the Langholm Project finished in 1997. The Langholm population fell back to two pairs. Breeding on the reserve was more likely well inside the reserve rather than around the boundaries. Another change came in the black grouse population. The addition of several plantations in the 1980s meant that black grouse were finally finding areas to feed, well away from sheep. A peak count of males showed 26, lekking in view of my house. There were few females with these males, though, and this population declined again after poor breeding seasons.

A major habitat was needed to give a boost to black grouse numbers and a Forestry Commission grant scheme enabled the society to plant over 110,000 native trees between 2004 and 2005, in an area of 570 acres on the side of Tindale Fell. This took the name of the old Bruithwaite Forest which once stretched from Forest Head to Wood End Farm. The main species of tree planted here were birch, hawthorn, rowan and holly, with plantings in the 1980s also including aspen, cherry, oak and mixed conifers. The understory of the one on Tindale Fell, now 20 years old, has naturally shaded out most of the bracken and replaced it with broad buckler fern, wood sorrel and grasses.

Money was also coming into the farm from government stewardship schemes which were started to encourage better management of farmland around Britain. The two largest farms, Geltsdale and Tarnhouse, had previously been drained high up in the peat so, instead of burning the heather, a cutting regime was started using bales of heather to block the drains and allow sphagnum to grow again, keeping the moor wet. This in turn would reduce the growth of heather so less cutting, if any, would be needed in the future.

Malcom Stott moved on in 2003 and Dave O'Hara arrived to become the manager. This was an historic moment for the reserve as Dave had started as a volunteer while I was there. Now he was running the reserve. Permanent staff numbers increased, with a farm manager and an upland manager, along with seasonal staff looking for hen harriers.

An old ruined semi-detached house, Stagsyke, was turned into offices and a visitor centre. Staff numbers still increased and a teacher was employed on a three-year contract. This was only the second time the reserve had employed a teacher – I had had one in the 1980s, again under a job creation scheme, working in local schools and giving the children wildlife tours, especially in Lower Gelt Wood.

Several small areas around the reserve were added for black grouse and wader habitat. Moorland on Tottergill (the valley of the fox) was bought in 2001, along with part of Talkin Fell in 2004 and part of Whinney Fell in 2005. A new shooting estate was created in 2010, adjoining the west end of the reserve, with new acquisitions drying up.

Things also changed on the south side of the reserve at Geltsdale Farm. Stewardship was paid to reduce sheep numbers to a point where a new agreement took all the sheep off the 6,000 acres. Cattle were to become the main grazers and it was hoped that trees would establish naturally rather than being planted. A small planting scheme had been tried in the 1990s with very little success, as trees were planted in the wrong places and with no extra management to look after them.

The first obvious result was the recovery of vole numbers around the fell. This in turn encouraged owls, with up to five pairs of barn owl at one time. Rabbit numbers, too, increased, bringing yet another species of owl to breed at Geltsdale. In 2009 a pair of eagle owls nested in the Gelt. This is a species yet to be classified as native but a pair in Yorkshire were allowed to rear 23 young before they were exposed to the public. Neither of these Geltsdale adults were ringed or had jesses on them so they had probably come from pairs nesting well out of the way of the public.

There was some concern about the eagle owls' effect on other breeding birds of prey, especially the hen harrier. A camera was placed on a harrier nest elsewhere in Lancashire and proved that there seemed to be no threat to other birds, especially as the camera confirmed that rabbits made up most – at times as much as 90% – of the prey items. The Geltsdale birds were no different. Pellets were collected and analysed and although there were some surprises, such as stoat and woodcock, there was no evidence of birds of prey. Pheasant and red grouse were also found but, surprisingly, no black grouse, even though this population was now increasing in the area.

In the two years the birds were present they managed to raise four chicks. In 2010 the government was asked if they should be culled but this was declined, as no damage to native species had been observed. The minister who made the decision was a shooting man and he probably realised that if eagle owls nested on shooting estates they could very well soon disappear anyway. Sadly, in 2011, this proved to be the case. My son Ewan saw the adult birds late into 2010, roosting well away from the nest site, but no display calls were heard in January and February (the female lays eggs at the end of February).

Other species of owls continued to survive after two very cold winters on the reserve, with short-eared owls making double figures in 2011. A pair of long-eared owls nested in a magpie's nest right outside my house, only 40 yards from a barn owl nest. The long-eared owl reared two young while the barn owl reared four. A kestrel nesting in a crow's nest only 100 yards from the long-eared owl failed due to high winds.

The bad news was that the reserve had gone four years without any hen harriers nesting, even with such a high number of voles for them to feed on. The good news was that black grouse peaked at 45 cocks, a rise from only seven in 2006. During bad weather in 2010 I could watch from my house as the birds fed on birch buds, while 400 red grouse had nothing to feed on in deep snow. A staggering 57 hens (known as greyhens) were counted that winter. Many of the birds moved in from neighbouring moors due to the lack of trees to feed on. This is getting close to the target of 50 males, set in 2008 when a whisky firm launched a new brand, Black Grouse, alongside its Red Grouse label. Money from the sale of this new whisky was to go to help this rare bird.

Dave O'Hara moved on in 2009 and was replaced by Steve Westerberg, the former farmland manager for the reserve.

Geltsdale has certainly had its ups and downs over the years. The future, I am sure, will very much depend on future governments supporting wildlife for the enjoyment of the public, alongside a new Langholm-style project producing enough hen harriers to come back and breed without being deterred by neighbouring estates.

Honey Buzzard

The Crags

The 19 miles from Greenhead to Chollerford offer some of the most spectacular scenery and history in the area. It is hard to grasp that, millions of
years ago, these crags were formed by the movement of tectonic plates, allowing
igneous rock to come to the surface. The Romans certainly made great use of
them to create their defensive wall and modern-day quarries are to be found
along this section too.

Walltown Crags (NY670660), managed by the Northumberland National
Park, seems a great place to start. Roman and modern quarrying have left a small
area of open ground colonized by orchids, maybe not with the feel of Gowk
Bank but easier to find, with little vegetation to obscure your views. Species like
northern marsh, common spotted and twayblade grace the quarry flora list, while
colonizers like coltsfoot and yellow rattle share the floor. One rare grassland fern,
adder's tongue, has also been found here.

Two small stretches of water allow species like mallard, coot and little grebe
to use the area, while pied wagtail and wheatear enjoy the openness of the quarry.
Following the footpath to rejoin the Wall, a piece of what can only be described
as parkland lies to the east – grassland with scattered trees, some of which have
been coppiced. Just as you enter the field, look to your right at the girth of the ash
tree closest to you. This tree is hundreds of years old and kept alive by coppicing.

The steep climb back to the Wall gives amazing views of the surrounding
countryside and some of the tallest sections of the remaining Wall are located just
along from here. The natural cliff here contains natural woodland of birch, hazel
and ash, with both redstart and cuckoo using the area, along with tree pipit (the
cuckoo lays its egg in the pipit's nest). A drained bog, once enjoyed by snipe and
curlew, lies below you to the north.

Above: Walltown Crags

Below: View over Walltown Crags

The SSSI of Allolee (NY686669) has a mixture of plant species growing on the whin sill. The rarest is wild chives, thought to have been brought here by the Romans defending the Wall. The Latin for this plant is *allium* and it grows on the downward (lee) side of the crags, giving rise to the name Allolee. Other species include many annual plants, the soil on these outcrops of rock often being very shallow. Some are quite rare, like hairy sedum, common whitlow grass and parsley piert, thyme and long-stalked cranesbill. Several sedges are found in a wet area below the crag, with spring and flea sedge worth looking for. Lichens are found on the exposed rock and the grassland is open to invasion from natural trees.

This invasion of trees on a unique habitat has led to the launch by the Northumberland Wildlife Trust of their own scheme to try and save places like this. It aims to develop the unique grasslands of Hadrian's Wall and the whin sill corridor, and enhance the nature and culture of what is a World Heritage Site and an important geological feature. This is part of their Living Landscape project, aiming to protect threatened red data book species such as wild chives, spignal, angular solomon's seal and spring cinquefoil.

Cawfields (NY713667) is another worked quarry with a small water area. There is less vegetation here but northern marsh orchid is found, although it seems well trampled by human feet.

By far the most photographed area of these crags is from Steele Rigg (NY751677) running onto Cuddy Crags with Crag Lough below it. This is one of the largest sections along the Wall with whin sill cliffs. Rock climbing takes place here as there is easy access from the minor road to the car park. One plant thought to have been brought here by the Romans is ground elder, once used as a salad but today thought of by gardeners as a very unwelcome weed. A large clump is found in the corner of the garden at Peel, overlooking the Wall.

The size of the crags here allows several bird species to come into their own, using the thermals to rise up over the Wall and away to hunt. Peregrine falcons, the fastest birds on the planet, use the crags to roost, along with kestrels, a smaller version of the peregrine, also known as the windhover. The crags could well have had breeding golden eagle and raven in Roman times. Jackdaws are the most common breeding bird here, along with stock dove, while wheatears and pied wagtails use the crags to catch insects. Some natural regeneration of trees has taken place, allowing redstarts to use the woodland, while crossbills have been found in the Scots pine plantation on top of the crag.

Reduced grazing has brought about a flourish of plants along this section. The yellow flowers of the beautiful rock rose shine out, even growing on the Wall itself. Thyme is everywhere, giving off its amazing scent underfoot. Clumps of heath bedstraw are starting to show, having been grazed down close to the ground. Both sheep's sorrel and common sorrel help to feed the finches like linnet and

63

Above: Steele Rigg

Below: Ground elder by Steele Rigg

goldfinch, while the extra-thick grasses help to protect the nests of meadow pipit, skylark and even curlew, the symbol of the Northumberland National Park where this site is found.

Not all the outcrops are found along the Wall, and exposed areas can often be seen in the distance. West Crindledyke quarry (NY781670), run by the Northumberland Wildlife Trust, is south of the Wall off the Bardon Mill to Crindledyke road. There is a lime kiln on the roadside indicating that the quarry was used for limestone extraction. This site is sometimes used by little owl with a mixture of lime-loving plants like salad burnet, felwort (autumn gentian) and crested hair grass.

Sowingshields Crags (NY800700) have a wide selection of plants like fairy flax, goldenrod, knapweed and autumn gentian, but the most amazing sight is the badger sett to the right of the farm (NY817706). The badgers had dug into the Vallum, upsetting English Heritage so much that they paid for large areas of it to be covered in thick netting, with only the entrances left open. This was supposed to prevent the badgers making any new holes in the Vallum. I have seen what badgers can chew through, including a security fence at a nuclear installation when a tasty dead sheep happened to lie on the other side. Badgers can outwit even military police.

65

Raven

The Chollerford bean field

Beans were first found in Afghanistan and appeared in the Mediterranean before the Roman Empire. So important were they as food that the Egyptians buried them in tombs so that the dead could rise in the afterlife and cultivate them again. This field can also be traced back to the Roman Empire, not by archaeology, but via a myth started by the Romans 2,000 years ago about a particular species of bird. They started killing this species – the owl – in a persecution which continues today.

This bean field tells a story of how predators can react to man's meddling in the ecosystem. Too often, modern man feels so dominant that, if something goes wrong, he has to react with a show of sheer strength, either by outright killing with a gun or with poisons which eventually affect the whole food chain.

And so to owls. A long-eared owl was nesting at the top of my drive, just 70 yards from my front door. To the Romans, it would have been a harbinger of death and the owl would have been killed and nailed to the door to ward off evil spirits. A barn owl was nesting 40 yards from the long-eared owl and tawny owls were in the garden. If I'd been a Roman, I would have felt that death was on its way.

A visitor told me the Chollerford story. Due to bad weather, a 30-acre (12½ hectare) field of beans was not harvested and went to waste. As beans are good food for rodents, an amazing number of rats, mice and voles came to the field and started to breed. Many predators – especially the barn owl, now restricted to around 4,000 pairs in the UK – then came to the field to feed on this bonanza.

One of the restrictions on the increase of this species is a lack of nesting sites. As the name suggests, this species once used man-made nest sites on farms. Modern buildings often do not offer suitable sites for nesting and old barns are often converted into homes for Britain's expanding population. Fortunately, around this field were many old, hollow ash trees used by jackdaws to nest. By adding plenty of sticks to make their nests, they also made trees suitable for many other species like the barn owl, the tawny owl, the kestrel and stock dove.

The staggering number of rodents allowed six pairs of barn owls to nest around the field that next year, a large percentage of the total number nesting in Northumberland. So extreme was it that the local barn owl recorder never believed the story. As the food source was short-lived, the rodent numbers were bound to crash and with it would go the number of barn owls. The number of owls nesting the next year was not recorded but if you look at the way barn owls are used in other countries to control rodents, then a question has to be asked: 'Why is a country like Britain, home to one of the world's largest bird charities, not using barn owls to reduce rodent numbers, especially around built-up areas?'

The next example happened to the north of the Wall, near Otterburn. A farmer had placed nest boxes on his farm to encourage barn owls to breed. He had one pair nesting every year and the local barn owl recorder would come and ring the young birds. Inspecting his nest box one day, the farmer found five dead chicks and was so upset that he sent the bodies away to be analysed to see what had killed them.

He was mortified to find that he had killed the young birds himself. Even though he had the owls on site feeding on his rodents, he had put out rat poison to reduce the numbers further. From that day on, no poison was used on the farm. The following year the barn owls produced six healthy youngsters. If the farmer needs to remove any rodents he uses humane traps and puts out the dead animals for the barn owls to feed on.

The moral of this story is that, even in modern times, we, like the Romans, are killing the predators we love by breaking up the food chain. Of course we have to protect ourselves from rodents, but there is a natural solution which relies on these rodents and which in turn helps us. One of the most common reasons for an explosion of rodents in urban gardens is bird feeding. Councils react to the problem by using poison and so the whole system breaks down. And it is not only barn owls whose numbers are low: kestrels have declined by 50% in some areas. Kestrels are well known for nesting in modern towns but barn owls could do so as well. In the Middle East barn owls have nested in Cairo, a city of more than 20 million people, and in other cities, using the minarets on mosques as nesting sites. No effort has ever been made in our towns to encourage these owls into built-up areas.

Two examples of control by farmers can be seen in Israel and Malaysia. In Israel, a staggering 35% of agricultural output can be destroyed by rodents and the poisons used can enter the food chain, affecting humans. The rodents soon learn to stop eating the poison, leading the companies to try even stronger and tastier poisons. The use of poison in agriculture was widespread, killing barn owls and large numbers of resident birds of prey and migrants passing through the country. It is estimated that around 100 million birds of prey pass through the country each spring and autumn.

The solution came in the shape of nest boxes. Placed at a staggeringly high density compared with in Britain, there were in some cases as many as 20 boxes in 150 metres stretch of land, with 74% occupancy. The average was closer to 200–400 metres apart and researchers were inspecting 60 boxes in a day. The scheme was so successful that it was expanded into neighbouring countries like Jordan.

Amazingly, the old Roman superstition was found to be alive and well in Jordan and the evil owl was not at first welcome in the fields. Fortunately, though, once the farmers saw the results from those farms that had taken up the scheme, the 2,000-year old hatred of the bird started to fade and the owl was seen as a bringer of wealth rather than of death. The boxes were also used by kestrels, adding to the fight against the rodents and saving money on poison.

The first barn owl projects in Malaysia were targeted at palm oil plantations where rats were destroying the crops. Nest boxes were placed in the crop at such a density as to reduce this destruction and the scheme was so successful that it was extended to the rice paddies. This project was started by the Ministry of Agriculture for Malaysia and it is interesting to note that no such scheme is to be found in Britain, apart from on a small scale via owl charities.

In Britain, as in other countries, poison is affecting many species beyond the barn owl. Red kites reintroduced to Gateshead have been found killed by rat poisons. Kestrels are declining in our area. Mammals like polecats are being killed when attracted to farms, especially in winter, to feed on rodents. Weasels and stoats, foxes and even domestic cats are all at risk. Worse still, some areas have high concentrations of what are called tunnel traps which kill even more of these mammal predators, even though the polecat is supposed to be protected by law. On one estate close to the bean field, 68 polecats were killed by these traps in a single year, which might just explain the subsequent explosion of rats.

So the story of the bean field is an eye-opener. It shows how man can – if he chooses – encourage wildlife not just as a spectacle to be enjoyed by visitors to the Wall, but as a natural defence against rodents.

Grey Heron

The Loughs

This is the name given to lakes or tarns in this part of Northumberland. The word has its origins in Ireland and applies to just a small area around the Wall where the whin sill is found. The main group of waters include Greenlee, Broomlee, Crag Lough and Grindon. All have been designated European Special Areas of Conservation (SAC) and Sites of Special Scientific Interest (SSSI) for their wildlife.

Crag Lough (NY765680) may be the easiest to see from the car park at Steele Rigg but as you walk along the Wall you will have ideal views onto the lough, scooped out during the last Ice Age. This water is owned by the National Trust and is an SSSI. It has a willow carr and a large area of aquatic vegetation around its fringes, including marsh cinquefoil, water forget-me-not, bog bean and water mint.

The breeding birds are slightly limited, with mute swan, little grebe, tufted duck, mallard, teal, water rail and coot. Winter sees goldeneye, whooper swan, grey heron, goosander and pochard using the 18-acre area, with a rare record of smew. A brown trout fishery operates here.

The two loughs to the north are very rarely watched for birds but still have an interesting list of species using them. They are designated for their plant life. Greenlee (NY770696) has an upland reed bed standing at 240 metres above sea level and its edge is one of the 58 border mires, so the plants can range from the normal wetland species like ragged robin, meadow sweet, sneezewort, valerian and yellow flag to peat-loving species like cranberry, sundew, cotton grass and bog asphodel.

Like many of these mires, drainage ditches have had to be filled up to keep the area wet and a boardwalk has been erected to allow access to view the bog. Curlew

Milefort & Crag Lough

and lapwing can both feed and breed here, as well as snipe and reed bunting, but it is the reed bed that attracts the rarer species of bird. In recent summers, marsh harriers have passed through the area, hunting the mire and roosting in the reed bed. This species has only just become a breeding bird in Northumberland. In winter the species changes to hen harrier, which come to the reed bed for a safe roosting site well out of the way of foxes.

Both sedge warbler and water rail nest in the reeds and both great crested grebe and mute swan have used the cover to build their nests too. Another summer visitor to the area has been osprey, with up to three birds seen fishing this shallow water. Like Tindale Tarn, the maximum depth is as little as 6 feet (2 metres), offering ideal fishing in most of the area. A small heronry is found on the south side of the lough where an osprey actually summered, using one of the old nests. A spotted crake was another interesting bird once heard calling here.

It is hard to imagine this tranquil area was once home to a yacht club, but the clubhouse is still on the shore and is now home to nesting swallows. Otters are common here, even in the daytime, and a hide has been erected by the National Park on the north side of the lough. Other mammals commonly seen here include fox, roe deer and stoat.

Winter brings another aspect to the water, with geese becoming common. Both Canada and greylag geese use the fields on the north side of the lough to graze and I have even seen Greenland white-fronted here, having moved over from Grindon, their main wintering site. Occasionally, whooper swans will visit the area but are less likely to stay now that free food is on hand on the Solway. Duck numbers can build up with mallard, teal, pochard, wigeon, goosander and goldeneye, but they are nowhere near as high as at Grindon.

Broomlee Lough (NY790698) is just off the Pennine Way, a national walk of 268 miles which makes the Hadrian's Wall Path look very short! Like Greenlee, this water is famous for its population of white-clawed crayfish. It is very hard to imagine the American species, which is devastating the rest of Britain, making it to these lonely loughs.

A famous former resident here was a red-necked grebe. This lonely male stayed for several summers, calling and driving off the local great crested grebes. It is a very rare breeding bird in Britain, with only one or two possible summering pairs per year. I was able to watch the bird in the early 1990s and at that time it was the only summering bird I had ever seen.

Distance makes it hard for most birdwatchers to cover the site but it has had more geese grazing and passing over than has Greenlee. Both barnacle and pink-footed pass over in the autumn and Greenland white-fronted geese sometimes use the area. Breeding birds are very similar to Greenlee but herons sometimes nest in the short willows out in the marsh, very different from the tall pines at Greenlee. A gull roost consisting of big gulls like herring, lesser black-backed and greater black-backed, can sometimes use the water.

73

Between these two loughs is an area of heather moorland. Adders are quite common here and there have been occasional sightings of merlin, rough-legged buzzard and goshawk. The small crags here have had nesting raven, and even snow bunting has been seen passing through the area, along with twite.

Grindon Lough (NY804676) is the most watched of all these loughs, as a minor road runs along its southern side looking down at the water. In a great demonstration of the Tyne Gap migration, several very rare species have been seen here over the years, including Wilson's phalarope, pectoral sandpiper, Caspian gull, green-winged teal and stone curlew.

Its summer bird used to be breeding black-necked grebe but fluctuating water levels mean that its host, the black-headed gull, has trouble nesting here in numbers. The gulls help to protect the grebe from predation so the grebe will only nest where the gulls are nesting in numbers and with the right vegetation. Waders are the main breeding birds here, with lapwing, redshank, oystercatcher, curlew and snipe.

Winter brings exciting numbers of duck to the area, mainly wigeon and teal, but shoveler, pintail, gadwall and mallard all use the area in small numbers. Rarer duck include smew, scaup and long-tailed duck. The geese are often the main attraction as they can draw in several species of passing birds. Canada geese make up the main numbers, with around 600, with smaller numbers of greylag geese, some of which have been linked with Icelandic birds.

A small flock of Greenland white-fronted geese have used the area for a number of years but still they struggle to make double figures each year. Pink-footed are sometimes mixed in with the Canada geese who often feed separately from the greylags. Barnacle geese have also stayed over to feed, but both of these pass through in their thousands in the autumn, heading for the Solway and Ribble estuaries. A small flock of tundra bean geese have also been found here, while a single snow goose was a great surprise one year.

Passage waders all depend on the amount of mud showing but black-tailed godwit, dunlin, ringed plover, ruff, green sandpiper and greenshank move through most years. Wintering waders can include lapwing and golden plover but with all these birds present, the site has also been a good location to look for birds of prey, with goshawk, peregrine falcon, hen harrier and buzzard.

Just to the south side of this road, a pair of Montagu's harriers nested in 2006. This was a very rare occurrence in the area: to see a single bird is a red letter day, but to see a pair with a second female must have been an amazing find this far north. The pair settled and eggs were thought to have been laid. The birds were often seen hunting over Grindon and its surrounding fields but, sadly, the eggs disappeared in suspicious circumstances and the female moved on. The male was seen around the Wall area for a number of weeks and it was hoped that they had tried again closer to Greenlee, but there were no more sightings.

Farther east along the Wall are man-made reservoirs which are the main water bodies, made to supply water to urban Newcastle. Colt Crag (NY9378) and Hallington reservoir (NY9776) are close together and both used for fishing. The number of bird species found on these two waters depends on the amount of coverage given to the areas by birdwatchers. Several interesting species have been seen, including black-tailed godwit, common scoter, rough-legged buzzard and smew at Colt Crag, while smew, dunlin, snow and tundra bean goose have been seen at Hallington.

Breeding great crested grebes are common at Colt Crag, while wintering duck at Hallington include wigeon, teal and mallard. Both have conifer woodland planted around them so siskin, redpoll and crossbills can be found, along with roe deer, red squirrels, otters and badgers. Small-fruited yellow sedge is an unusual plant of the area.

To the north-east of here lies another man-made water called Sweethope Lough (NY940825) with its water falling into the Wansbeck. This is also used for fishing but several times in recent years has attracted osprey to enjoy the rainbow trout. Some interesting birds include passing common crane, whooper swan and nightjar.

All the water from the reservoirs runs into another set of reservoirs at Whittle Dean (NZ065684), found on the Hadrian's Wall Path. The site has a bird hide (the only one along the path) and a picnic table. The hide is accessible from the Military Road (B6318) but the parking is very poor. A combination of easy access and a location on the flight path of the Tyne Gap has meant that around 200 bird species have been identified at this site. Water birds have included both red-throated and great northern divers, Slavonian and red-necked grebe. The wintering flock of wigeon managed to attract a drake American wigeon, while the deep water has had many diving ducks including ferruginous, ring-necked, long-tailed, scaup and even eider inland.

Depending on the grain in the local fields, whooper swans can winter here. Even Bewick's swan has been seen, so close to the home at Cherryburn of the man who named it. There is a long list of goose species, with both forms of white-front-ed, taiga bean and barnacle standing out. Birds of prey include honey buzzard – a species which is hard to find in the county – hobby and marsh harrier. A male osprey summered here in 2007, often perching in a tree in easy view of the hide.

Waders again point to the migration through the Tyne Gap, with many coastal birds like turnstone, sanderling, knot, bar-tailed godwit and purple sandpiper turning up here, along with species which prefer fresh water, like Temminck's stint, wood sandpiper, black-tailed godwit and ruff. The green sandpiper has wintered here, using a side stream off the B6309 to Stamfordham. Rarer American waders like white-rumped and pectoral sandpiper have been found, along with avocet and curlew sandpiper.

Both kittiwake and Arctic skua are good examples of the Tyne Gap migration, along with several terns including marsh terns like black- and white-winged tern. Always worth finding in spring are the yellow wagtails, this being a hotspot for them, along with records of the Scandinavian form, blue-headed. The trees around the reservoir have held wood warbler, pied flycatcher and redstart, along with many more passage birds.

If this was the reservoir built for Newcastle, then Derwent Reservoir is for Gateshead. An attractive circular drive can take in several locations starting at Corbridge and its Roman town of Corstopitum. The fort was centred on two Roman roads, the Stanegate and Dere Street, coming up from York. It was also the crossing point of the Tyne, not to mention the last stop-off for boats up the Tyne.

The easiest way to find the reservoir is to drive back east along the A69 and take the A68 south over the river. Rise up until you see the first brown signs for the reservoir, taking the minor road at NZ039552. Take the next left, dropping down to the Millshield picnic site with access to the water. Here you can scan around the reservoir looking for wildfowl, waders and gulls. Some rare waders have been found here, such as pectoral, spotted and buff-breasted sandpipers. Look out for osprey or red kite and check the ducks for pintail, scaup or common scoter. Drive back to the minor road, turning left, and follow on along the reservoir with several spots to scan for wildlife in the area.

The minor road meets the B6306. Turn right, entering the medieval village of Blanchland, famous for its 12th-century abbey. You then rise up for a wonderful view back onto the reservoir. The road passes Slaley Forest (NY9655), famous for its summering nightjars and passing honey buzzards. The road then drops down to Dipton Wood, also planted with conifers, and over the Linnels Bridge, scene of the battle of Hexham, won by a Yorkist army in 1464 during the War of the Roses. You are soon in Hexham with its abbey built with the help of Roman stone. The circular route is complete, returning to Corbridge via the A69 to make a trip of roughly 50 miles.

76

Wigeon

Kielder

A shortage of timber during World War One brought legions of conifer trees, row upon regimented row, to the land where legions of Roman soldiers had once marched. The Forestry Commission was set up in 1919 and from 1920 the scene was set for what was at the time the largest man-made forest in Europe. The forest also paved the way for the creation of Europe's largest man-made stretch of water, the Kielder reservoir. During the 1930s the Ministry of Labour supplied men from among the great numbers of unemployed, many of whom came from the mining communities and shipyards of north-east England.

Before the coming of the trees, the Romans had come to the north Tyne for one special jewel: the pearl found in freshwater mussels. This rare mollusc now survives in only two locations in England but, worse still, the Tyne mussel is no longer breeding, thanks, it is thought, to the ploughing and fertiliser use associated with the creation of the forest.

The big dam which creates the reservoir means that migratory salmon and sea trout have to be helped – manhandled, in fact – into the upper water. The mussels' larvae lodge in the gills of these fish for several months before sinking into the sand of the river. Too much silt caused by the ploughing lines to plant the trees was choking the larvae and it is now hoped that captive-bred ones will bring new life back into the river. If management can improve conditions there, then not only will the mussels thrive but so will the migratory fish and everything else in the river.

The forest itself is slowly becoming a tourist attraction. The same trees that made the area have become a home to rare wildlife. At the top of the list was golden eagle, which arrived here in 1972 but which, sadly, were kept a secret. Most birdwatchers knew about them but the general public did not, and the eagles themselves were not used as iconic creatures worth protecting.

In the early years a nest was built for them just on the Scottish side – for political reasons – of the border and wild goats were killed, both to protect the young trees in the forest and to feed the eagles. The dead goats were fed on by the female eagle in particular, keeping her in condition for egg-laying. So successful was this management that the nest often produced two young, with over 20 young reared during the nest's lifetime. Young birds moved out, especially into the borders of Scotland, where new pairs were created. Any which moved onto red grouse moors were destroyed, as happened in Lakeland.

In the end, this left few birds to help keep the population going, especially as the nest site was becoming prone to disturbance, and in many years no young were being reared at all. Disturbance at the nest site became a real problem even though the bird and its nest sites are specially protected by law. Even students working for their Duke of Edinburgh awards and mountain bikers were known to wander round the nest site. An exceptional year was 2001, the year of foot and mouth, when no-one was allowed to walk in the countryside. A single female chick was produced which wandered around the north Pennines near Alston until it was destroyed.

In the last breeding season (2007) cameras and sound equipment were used to find out what was going on with this pair. Sadly, the male was thought to have been caught in a crow trap and was never seen again. The female kept incubating the eggs but in the end had to give up as there was no male to bring food to her. She was last seen in 2008 when she moved over to Peebles and found another mate on territory.

Today no breeding birds remain. All the Border eagles have been removed by shooting interests, leaving no birds to recolonise the site. The fact that they were kept a secret was their downfall. There are only 200,000 visitors a year to the area yet how many more would have come to see these magnificent birds if they had been managed properly? Surely the income these birds would have created would have paid for any protection measures?

A public raptor-viewing point in Kielder had a display board showing which birds of prey could be seen in the area of the forest. The only species present but not shown was the eagle. The forest today takes great pleasure in shouting about its newest arrivals, the ospreys, but what a great shout it would have been for this giant of birds.

Ospreys came to Cumbria to breed in 2001 (the year of foot and mouth) and to Kielder in 2009. Again a nest was built for the birds and in their first year they raised three chicks. 2010 saw three more and in 2011 two pairs raised a chick each. In 2010 the second pair had tried to breed in a nest they had built themselves but had failed, probably due to their inexperience at nesting. They used the same tree in 2011 but with plenty more sticks and pieces of string, courtesy of forestry rangers.

A website gives information about the birds and a live camera beams pictures back to Kielder Castle visitor centre. How wonderful it would have been had the same been done for the eagles. Boat trips on the reservoir offer sightings of the ospreys, as do telescopes – with volunteers on hand to help – at Leaplish Waterside Park, part of the reservoir.

The forest is famous for two other birds, the goshawk and the tawny owl. The goshawk loves to nest in the thick spruce trees, which also hold a lot of its prey: wood pigeons, crows and the occasional red squirrel. Come winter, many of the goshawks move down onto lower ground looking for food, where they come up against large numbers of pheasants put out for shooting. Sadly, many of the goshawks are killed, leaving many immature birds to carry on the breeding. Goshawks are best observed in February and March when they start their display to cement their territories. The raptor viewpoint at Bakethin (NY636910) is a great place to start for anyone wanting to observe this species.

The tawny owls, on the other hand, have many boxes erected for their use. As many as 200 boxes cover the 155,000 acres of the forest, with over 100 pairs using the boxes in good vole years. As a nocturnal species it may not be the easiest bird to see, but its boxes are now also being used by a species normally found in China, the Mandarin duck.

This duck has escaped from private collections and has spread to many locations in Britain. The hollow trees in which it normally nests are very rare, especially in a modern conifer plantation, but when folk go out of their way to add boxes for another species then others might join in to use them for themselves. A great place to see this duck is on the north Tyne just below the Kielder Dam at Falstone Bridge (NY723871). In recent years, these boxes have also helped barn owls to flourish, rising from two pairs in 1999 to 25 pairs in 2008. The bad winters in 2009–2010 and 2010–2011 left this species with no breeding birds, which was not the picture further west in Cumbria.

There are many more species in the forest than there were when it was a moorland area. Crossbills enjoy the crops of cones produced by the trees: find the cone and you usually find the bird. Siskin also like this harvest and are very common around the forest.

The one raptor whose numbers have fallen fast is the merlin. Its open habitat has been replaced by trees but, given that it normally nests in old crow and raven nests in the rest of its world range, it flourishes around the edge of the forest, having changed its diet from pipits to crossbill and siskin. One theory for its decline is the lack of nest sites, as crow numbers decreased with the arrival of the goshawk and the buzzard. Buzzards have also been found feeding on the young of the merlin. To reduce the numbers of buzzards you need the top predator in the sky, the golden eagle.

The mammal which the public most often want to see is the red squirrel. Here there is little food for the grey squirrel which has taken over in most of Britain. This conflict of food has meant that large seed-producing trees like oak and beech have not been planted in the forest. Fine seed like that of the conifers, birch and alder does not feed the grey squirrel so the red is well at home here.

The top predator of squirrels, the pine marten, is missing. It would have an effect not just on squirrels but on the tawny owls as well, as it needs hollow trees to make its den and the owl boxes would be ideal for them. Other mammals present here include foxes, roe deer, badgers, stoats, weasels and bats.

Another habitat often hidden by the trees is the blanket bog. Blanket bogs or border mires were sometimes drained by forestry operations and planted up with trees. Over and around the area of these new plantations, 58 bogs have been identified in Cumbria and Northumbria. Falstone Bog, a Northumberland Wildlife Trust reserve, is found close to the dam. It is the plants which make this area special with sphagnum mosses keeping the site wet, acting as a sponge, soaking up all the water and holding it, even during dry periods. Growing around these are cotton grasses, bog asphodel, cranberry and bog rosemary. These bogs are good for dragonflies, especially black darter, which loves the acid conditions.

80

Red Kite

Hadrian's kite project

The red kite was once found throughout the UK, but during the 19th century most birds were removed by shooting estates. Only a small number remained, in Wales, but these birds were non-migratory. Since then there have been several successful reintroductions of red kite in the UK, over several years, but most of these birds also remained in the area where they were released.

Red kites feed mainly on carrion, with road kills, especially rabbits and pheasants, being an easy source of food. They do not compete with other birds of prey like buzzards, which have actually been seen to increase, particularly in the release areas, thanks to a reduction in persecution due to the presence of kites. Rabbits are also a food item, which the Romans may have released into the British countryside as a source of meat for themselves.

The red kite is a very appealing bird to look at and has been accepted by most people in the areas of release, with many even leaving out scraps in their gardens as food. The red kite has quickly become a symbol of something greater than itself, involving whole communities in its success.

In Roman times the bird was probably found all along the Wall, scavenging around settlements as it does today. Kite remains have been found, especially in Carlisle. Most modern-day reintroductions are based in open country areas but the Gateshead reintroduction ('Northern Kites') took place in a mainly urban area in view of the Wall. Although classed as urban, Gateshead has a range of wooded valleys like the Derwent Valley which could offer the birds easy breeding conditions. Most of these were managed either by the National Trust (Gibside) or Forestry Commission (Chopwell) with smaller areas like Ryton Willows and Thornley Woods managed by Gateshead Council.

The Gateshead Kite project took place between 2004 and 2009, with all young birds being brought from another reintroduction area, the Chilterns in southern England. The young were picked from successful nests with more than one chick. This Chiltern population had expanded so fast, with over 300 pairs, that it provided kites for several reintroduction schemes. In total, 94 kites were released in a three-year period with 20 birds in 2004, 41 in 2005 and 33 in 2006. Extra years were spent looking for breeding success and increasing awareness of the birds and the environment in over one million people living within a 20-minute radius of the release site.

Like everything in life, this scheme had to be paid for and the main finance came from Gateshead Council itself. This meant that the public in that area were paying for the scheme via their council tax. Other money was found via Natural England, a government organisation again funded by the taxpayer. The Forestry Commission also helped out with their public woodland, along with two public charities, the RSPB and the National Trust, one with expertise in birds and the other owning land in the release area. Northumbria Water also helped out. Funding also came from SITA, a private company which passed on money raised via the landfill tax. It is interesting to note that not only did money come from SITA, but that the red kites fed on the very rubbish tips which they were charging businesses to use.

With these financial backers in place, money was also obtained from the Heritage Lottery Fund. Staff were employed via Gateshead Council under the banner 'Northern Kites' and an office and release pens were made available. These were situated in the lower Derwent valley with a view across the surrounding countryside so that the young kites could learn to recognise their new home. The pens were also placed in sites away from public pressure to reduce disturbance at a critical stage in their new lives.

The birds were not brought to this area just for the benefit of birdwatchers: the idea was to use them to encourage more people to get out into green areas and walk for the good of their physical and mental health. Blood pressures have been tested in a woodland setting and lower readings found in people walking there than along city streets. For a big urban area like the north-east, the birds were to act as doctors and nurses.

Walks were designed in the area using a kite logo and the Kite Trail, a 17-mile route with its own unique waymark, was widely publicised. It is a circular walk with many sections suitable for wheelchairs and buggies. There are several bus stops along the way so the whole walk does not have to be done in one go. Nine of the buses, bearing the red kite symbol, travel out from the city centre as far as Consett. There are sections suitable for bikes, with the coast-to-coast cycle route (Whitehaven–Sunderland) following a part of the Kite Trail, and even horse riding allowed along some of its length. There are several different habitats, including woodland, wetland and open countryside, and the Derwent Walk Country Park is situated on the trail, offering several historic buildings and a nine-arched viaduct.

Schools were to use the birds to learn about the environment. Individual schools were allocated individual birds and coloured wing tags allowed the birds to be identified away from the pens. Information would then be given to the schools on what the birds were doing and, in their later years, even about their nesting success.

The kite reintroduction as a whole, although costing money, was in fact intended to generate cash, with trails passing close to shops and pubs. Visitors to the area would spend locally and even a beer – Wylam Brewery's Northern Kite ale – was named after the project, adding to publicity for the scheme. Local artists use the symbol of the kite in paintings, greetings cards, glass sculptures, photographs and carvings. The scheme was mentioned in the Houses of Parliament and ministers came to see the project in action.

The first breeding birds were found in Gateshead, with the two young hatched and confirmed on 12 June 2006, and the first in Northumberland came in 2007. These represented the first young to fly from a nest in the north-east of England in over 170 years. These young were also wing tagged to allow them to be identified as they moved around the area. The mother of one of the chicks hatched in Northumberland, again identified by her unique coloured wing tags, had spent some of the summer of 2006 in Perthshire.

The wing tags have shown that a number of these released birds have travelled around the country, with birds located in areas where other releases have taken place, such as Yorkshire, the Chilterns, Worcestershire and the Highlands of Scotland. One Yorkshire bird released on the Harewood Estate near Harrogate came the other way, arriving in the area to breed with a local bird.

Movement around Durham and Northumberland has not been without its problems. When the birds are given to schools they are also given a name so, for example, Flash belonged to Winlaton West Lane community primary school. The bird had also had a transmitter added to the wing tag, to allow his movements to be followed more closely. It was released in July 2004 and by August had moved to Prudhoe, then by October to Plenmeller near Haltwhistle.

The transmitter showed that the bird had stopped moving, which seemed to indicate that it had died. The police were called to help locate the bird and, sure enough, poor Flash was lying dead with what turned out to be a poisoned rabbit and pheasant close by his corpse. Four months later a press conference was called to announce the death and condemn this illegal act which robbed the school of its prize bird. The story made the national newspapers and TV but still the kites were under pressure from shooting estates.

Some of the kites were able to settle in the Tees valley, 35 miles south-west of their release site near Barnard Castle. Breeding was confirmed but, like Flash, the birds were removed from the area, although no carcasses were found. In 2010, closer still to the release site, a breeding pair was killed with rodenticide. This poison is put out by man to kill rats, the very thing the kites take as prey. Not only were the adults dead, but the nest contained young, which would have perished where they lay.

This followed on from another death of two more birds on Hexhamshire Common. Even fitted with wing tags and transmitters, red kites are going missing and the Gateshead birds are struggling to move out to new areas to colonise.

These last deaths also bring into question the very same council who put so much time and money into bringing back the red kites in the first place. Gateshead City Council, like every other council in Britain, uses pest controllers to remove unwanted rats and mice from people's homes or from industrial work places. This poison is supposed to be laid in a safe way, so that no other predators can find the poisoned animals after their death.

Red kites are feeding around many of these properties, to the extent that some people put food out to encourage them to visit their gardens. In one case, a lady placed a poisoned mouse in a bag which she put on the dustbin, meaning to dispose of it later. The wind blew the bag onto the lawn, exposing the mouse, and she saw a red kite fly down and take it.

The chances of these poisoned mammals getting into the food chain are immense. Recent examination of dead red kites, kestrels and barn owls show that many carry poison in their liver. The liver's job is to flush out drugs and toxins but it can only take so much. As the main poison used is an anticoagulant, internal bleeding eventually takes place, killing the bird. As many as 60% of all kestrels examined had this poison in their systems, even though the companies which sell it claim that it only goes to people who use it in a professional manner.

No-one wants to see plagues of rats and mice in our towns and cities but when many people act irresponsibly, feeding birds and disposing carelessly of general waste, especially household waste, then more rats and mice will be the result. No attempt was made by the Northern Kite project to tackle this problem and given that the scheme stopped in 2009, the Northumberland and Tyneside Bird Club called for it to be extended to tackle problems like poisoning.

I myself tried to encourage another reintroduction in the Carlisle area to spread the kites along the Wall. As yet, it seems, no-one wants to listen, even though red kites have been reintroduced further south in Cumbria and are also being shot and poisoned, as these communities have not taken the birds to their hearts. A 'Friends of Red Kites' group has been set up in the north-east and in

2011 tried to influence people along the Tyne at Hexham to prevent the open poisoning of the birds.

So although schemes seem to have helped this iconic species back into people's lives, there is a long way to go before healthy red kites, free of poisons, fly safely along the Wall.

86

Waxwing

Above: Red squirrel

Top left: Sea Eagle with fish

Bottom left: Sea holly

Above: Grindon Lough

Above left: Short-eared owl

Below Left: Short-eared owl eggs

Left: Tawny owl

Right: Solway looking towards Criffel

Below: Talkin tarn

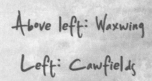

Above left: Waxwing

Left: Cawfields

Kittiwake city

Newcastle might not seem the obvious place to talk about a seabird colony, but lo and behold, with 20 kilometres still to go before reaching the sea, here is a colony of kittiwakes, the world's first inland.

The Tyne Bridge, joining Newcastle to Gateshead, was the world's longest single-span bridge when it was opened in 1928. Newcastle itself was the Roman fort of Pons Aelius (Bridge of Hadrian) but its modern name came from the 'new castle' built in 1080 by the Normans. Now it is home to part of this kittiwake colony.

Newcastle itself has been named Britain's greenest city two years in a row, so the kittiwakes must have known this was a great place to come and rear their young. The nearby Marsden Rock, just off the mouth of the Tyne, has had breeding kittiwakes for many years, with around 1,000 pairs in 1950. The population doubled in the 1960s but after this dramatic increase, numbers then rose more slowly until the early 1990s, when it reached 5,000 pairs, falling back to 2,000 in the late 1990s.

It was in 1949 that the first birds ventured up the Tyne to breed. By 1953 there were already 100 pairs using the buildings around the fish quay at North Shields. By 1965 they had moved further inland to a sheet metal factory at Gateshead and onto the Baltic flour mill. 1990 saw the Gateshead Flower Festival attract three million visitors to the area and 200 pairs of kittiwake used the mill to breed. The flour mill was spotted as a potential art gallery and from 1995–2002, £50 million was spent on converting it. Sadly, the kittiwakes were not seen as art and were removed.

In 1998, Gateshead Council erected an alternative nesting tower for the kittiwakes on Saltmeadows Park by the Tyne. So far, a maximum of 134 pairs have

Left: Tyne Bridge

Right: The Guildhall, Newcastle

taken up residence here, with other pairs having moved onto the north shore. One of the new locations was the famous Tyne Bridge. In 1997 two pairs nested here, with 13 pairs in 1998, and 39 pairs by 1999, rising to 82 pairs by 2002. In 2010 there were 250 pairs nesting on the bridge. Some pairs had moved onto the Guildhall, a listed building built in 1655. The local council installed spikes to stop them nesting, only to find that they nested behind them.

Other locations used in 2009 included International Paints at Hebbon with 113 nests and Tyne Docks (Redhead slipway) with 35 nests. Amazingly, despite the renovation of the Baltic flour mill, 30 pairs returned to nest on it. An interesting aspect of the choice of nest sites revolves around the view of the river. The kittiwake tower at Saltmeadows has three sides, facing east, west and south, but none directly facing the river. Birds nesting on the west side made up around 50% of the colony while 40% used the east side, but only 10% used the south, which looks directly away from the river.

The public have plenty of viewpoints from which to see the birds from March to the beginning of August. The Baltic flour mill now has cameras trained on the nests so it is possible to watch the development of the nest, eggs and chicks from the second floor. The kittiwake platform is another site to visit on the south side of the Tyne. Walking over the Tyne Bridge you can look down onto the birds nesting below, while even on the quayside there is a display board giving information about the birds to tourists and walkers.

The kittiwake was one of the birds mentioned in the very early Anglo-Saxon poem 'The Seafarer', written around 685 A.D. It was found in the Exeter Book, one of the finest examples of ancient literature. The poem was written during the time of the Venerable Bede, founder of the monastery at Jarrow on the south side of the Tyne. A dedication stone here is dated 685 A.D., the same date as the poem. It was probably in this era that kittiwakes were thought to be the reincarnation of children's souls, thanks to their calls.

Numbers of breeding birds at Marsden have fallen and it is not the only area in which populations have crashed. Northern Scotland once had a population of 54,600 pairs, now down to 23,000. Observers worried by this decline fitted kittiwakes with radio tracking devices so that their movements could be monitored, particularly during the breeding season. The data revealed that the birds can travel a maximum of 150 kilometres to look for food, with some birds travelling only a few kilometres from the nest. It is suspected that the food supply is the cause of this decline and future work will determine whether or not this is the case.

Closer to home, the breeding tower at Gateshead also allows the local Durham ringing group the chance to ring the chicks. This also provides information on the movement of the birds via the colour combinations of rings on their legs. Over a two-month period, two juveniles moved along the east coast north to Druridge Bay and North Berwick, while a juvenile ringed in 1988 was found alive at Bizkaia in northern Spain in February 2009, meaning that it had reached the great age of 21. Another bird was found in the Minch in western Scotland in its second year.

One of the early-nesting Tyne birds ringed at North Shields in 1960 travelled north to the northern coast of Iceland, where it was found a year later on the island of Flatey, having travelled 1,523 kilometres. Another bird ringed in 1967 was found sick on the island of Oland in Sweden at the age of 26, having entered the Baltic. This is only two years short of the oldest-ever recorded kittiwake found in Britain, which came from the Farne Islands, close by in Northumberland.

Satellite tracking has studied the winter movements of these birds as well as their summer behaviour. Eighty kittiwakes were tracked from the Isle of May in the Firth of Forth after their breeding success had been monitored. Birds that bred successfully wintered closer to home than birds that had failed to breed successfully. Birds that had failed left the nesting area early and travelled a staggering 3,000 kilometres across the Atlantic to winter off Canada. Is it the case that Tyne birds do the same?

The icing on the cake would be to have some of the Tyne birds satellite tagged so that they could be followed across the oceans, painting a complete picture of their movements. It would also be great if one of these tagged birds were to use the Tyne Gap, travelling across land through the Solway over the heads of the walkers on the Hadrian's Wall Path to its nest site on the Tyne. When sitting seawatching in the bus shelter at Bowness on Solway, I could then know that at least some of the birds passing overhead in their thousands were actually local birds and not simply travelling to nest sites high up in the Arctic.

Kittiwakes

Thomas Bewick

A book covering this area would not be complete without a word on one of the heroes of British natural history. Thomas Bewick has been described as Northumberland's greatest artist, wood engraver and naturalist. Born in 1753 in a small farmhouse called Cherryburn on the south side of the Tyne, he went to school across the river at Ovingham and by the age of 14 was signed up for seven years as an apprentice to an engraving business in Newcastle.

It was here that his boss, Ralph Beilby, noticed his talent and soon had him working on woodcuts. Thomas was soon working on children's books. Once his apprenticeship had finished he went on a 500-mile walkabout in Scotland, moving to London on his return but soon living back in Newcastle. His first big volume, *A General History of Quadrupeds*, was published in 1790. His knowledge of birds was helped by studying skins at Wycliffe Hall near Barnard Castle and *Land Birds*, his first volume of *History of British Birds* came out in 1797, followed by *Water Birds* in 1804.

Thomas died in 1824 leaving a wife and four children, none of whom had children of their own. Much of his work was taken up by the Hancock Museum in Newcastle via the Northumberland Natural History Society which is based there. A resurgence in interest in Thomas's work did not really begin until 1982 when his birthplace came up for sale. A trust was formed to buy the farmhouse and it was handed over to the National Trust in 1991.

A Bewick Society was formed in 1989 to promote a greater interest in Thomas's work.

Pied Flycatcher

Down the Tyne

O nce you have left the Whittle Dene reservoir, it does not seem long before you are in the heart of Newcastle. While around 100,000 people live on the west side of the Wall, you are now in an area with a population of more than 1.6 million. This has advantages and disadvantages for wildlife: councils will spend money on wildlife as a tool for recreation, but the very fact that land is built on takes away much of the 'wild' atmosphere felt further back along the Wall.

Gateshead, Newcastle, North Tyneside and South Tyneside councils have spent money on country parks and nature reserves, with footpaths and cycle ways to get you around the area. Many of these paths are historical wagon ways which were used to get the coal down to the docks. Over 400 miles of wagon ways existed around the area at the peak of the coal mining era, with many, including parts of the Hadrian's Wall Path and cycle route, now turned into walking and cycling routes.

With such a long industrial past, some of the new wildlife areas are former workings of coal, metal and associated industries. The 150-acre (60-hectare) Tyne Riverside Country Park at Newburn is just one of these areas. Based around the Hadrian's cycle way, this area offers a wide variety of wildlife as well as showing its industrial past. Both a coal mine (Isabella colliery) and the Newburn steel works were found here. The Wylam wagon way has been converted into the cycle track and George Stephenson was married in the local church, with his cottage two miles further back up the track in Wylam village. To view both sides of the river there is a 20-mile round cycle route covering this and the next wildlife site.

The habitats in the park include grassland, reed beds – added to clean the rusty water coming out of the mine – scrub and woodland, a large pond locally called the Reigh and the River Tyne itself. Mine shale and the coke ovens are all that is left of the old industrial days but these varied habitats allow wildlife to thrive. The fresh water found in the pond attracts large numbers of gulls to gather here to preen and roost. The Tyne is tidal at this section so this fresh water is a godsend for these birds and several hundred may be found here, including black-headed, herring and lesser black-backed, with common gull in winter. Rarer gulls like glaucous and Iceland gull have been found here.

Kingfishers are a great sighting on any day but the reed bed also provides nesting sites for reed warblers, which are a rare find on the west side of the Wall, along with sedge warbler and reed bunting. Several woodland species can be found, including nuthatch, marsh and willow tit, but the river adds passage birds, with waders like common sandpiper, oystercatcher, curlew and lapwing, some of which winter. Common terns hunt the river for small fish and do not be surprised to see grey seal this far up the river, often encouraged by the migrating salmon and sea trout which make the River Tyne one of the top game fishing rivers in Britain.

A wide variety of plants have taken over the industrial site, including the alpine pennycress which was found growing upstream on gravel contaminated by heavy metals, but at this location the helleborine growing with it is dune helleborine rather than the rarer Tyne variety. Other unusual plants include Smith's pepperwort and whorled water milfoil.

Across the river from here is the Ryton Willows reserve (NZ155650) created by the Gateshead Council with 106 acres (43 hectares). The ponds here are SSSIs due to their former botanical flora, with water plants such as bladderwort and frogbit now no longer found here. The ponds are just part of the reserve with mature woodland, grassland and, again, the River Tyne. The woodland has held all three species of woodpecker, with the lesser spotted now very rare in the area. Hawfinch is another great bird to find, along with the ever-present red kites patrolling the skyline.

The ponds themselves, used for the sport of curling in the era of continuous hard winters, have several breeding birds like mute swan, little grebe, coot and moorhen. Dragonflies are well worth looking for in the summer, with migrant, southern and common hawker along with emperor dragonfly and many damselflies. Bulrush, juncus, marsh cinquefoil, greater pond sedge and bladder sedge add to the edge effect of the ponds where you might find the discarded cases of the hatched nymphs of these remarkable insects.

The grasslands are often grazed by docile belted galloway cattle, adding to the colour of the flowers found here. Both meadow cranesbill and meadow scabious add nectar for the butterflies, which include wall, peacock, painted lady, red admiral, orange tip, small copper and small tortoiseshell. A large number of moths have been caught and identified here as well. The river vegetation includes sea aster, due to the salt from the tidal river here.

The Tyne at this point has regular cormorant and grey heron, along with winter arrivals of goosander and goldeneye, with rarer records of smew, black- and red-throated diver, common scoter and black-necked grebe. Otters are now seen using both the river and the ponds. Farm birds like yellowhammer, linnet and chaffinch add to the bird list along with summer warblers like lesser whitethroat and garden warbler.

Moving inland is the Derwent Walk country park now famous for its red kites, with two visitor centres at Thornley (NZ178604) and Swalwell (NZ198620). Again there is a range of habitats with many walks and cycle routes around the area, many of which are serviced by easy bus rides to get you to your starting point. The woodland has a wide range of birds, with occasional breeding pied flycatcher, redstart and wood warbler, but a good range of tits along with willow tit which can be best seen down at Far Pastures (NZ170590). A feeding station at Thornley allows you to get close views of many of the woodland birds, especially great spotted woodpecker and nuthatch.

There is a bird hide at Far Pastures which you need a key to enter. The key allows you access to several hides in the area, including Shibdon, and for £5 it is a real bargain. It can be obtained from the Thornley visitor centre (tel. 01207 545212) or via Gateshead council. The bird hide acts as a useful wildlife-watching shelter in wet weather but can also serve as a good base from which to photograph a wide range of species.

95

Far Pastures

Commoner species include kingfisher, water rail, grey heron and coot, with little grebe, moorhen and mallard available. Snipe and jack snipe are great winter classics, along with teal, gadwall and goldeneye. A number of rarer birds have turned up, with garganey, green-winged teal, red-rumped swallow, firecrest and little ringed plover. Birds flying through the Derwent Valley have included osprey, Montagu's harrier and common crane. The reed beds here can offer views of reed, sedge and willow warblers in summer, along with reed bunting and wren. Plants include water plantain.

The red kites managed to nest for the first time in the park and a large roost takes place here at Gibbs Side, opposite Far Pastures on the National Trust land across the River Derwent. The river itself offers grey wagtail, dipper and kingfisher. Goosanders breed occasionally, using hollow trees to nest in. The 17-mile red kite trail which is found in the park has several viewpoints at which to stop and watch the birds.

The 34 acres at Shibdon Pond (NZ195628) are under joint management between Gateshead council and Durham Wildlife Trust. Over 180 species of birds have been seen in the area, with many drawn in from the nearby River Tyne. A hide (for which you need a key) can be found in the south-west corner. Once the area was wetland grassland but now subsidence from coal mining has left it with stretches of open water and large areas of aquatic vegetation including reed, bulrush and willow scrub.

The birds have certainly brightened up the area and range from golden oriole, black-tailed godwit to green sandpiper, white stork, green-winged teal, red-throated diver, black tern and pink-footed goose. Many of these were passing through but many use the area to look for potential breeding sites. Mute swan, water rail, coot and moorhen all use the aquatic vegetation to build their nests. Spring and autumn passage may include garganey, spotted redshank, greenshank, spotted crake, ruff, little stint, common sandpiper, osprey and little egret.

The winter sees many duck come to the area to feed, including wigeon, teal, shoveler, pochard and tufted duck. The fresh water also encourages gulls to come here to preen and rest, with both Iceland and glaucous gull found, along with Mediterranean, yellow-legged and even a laughing gull from North America.

The wetland is good for dragonflies with nine species recorded and 15 species of butterfly. The flora is both in and out of the water, with water starwort, stonewort, reed sweet grass, greater pond sedge, broad-leaved helleborine, marsh and common spotted orchid, bee orchid and cuckoo flower feeding the larvae of the orange-tip butterflies. The big noctule bats have been seen here, feeding over the water, along with foxes hunting the many rabbits.

Crossing back over the river is Prestwick Carr (NZ185736). This is an area of wild grassland, wetland and hedgerows covering an area of 791 acres (320 hectares) on an urban fringe. It is well known for its birds of prey and owls, with all five species often found in the area. In 2004, a radio-tagged marsh harrier flew down from Tayside in Scotland via Carlisle and stayed three weeks on the Carr before moving south and into France. It was then tracked down through Spain and into Africa, wintering around Gambia and Senegal. A radio-tagged white-tailed eagle, also from eastern Scotland, stayed on the Carr for several days in 2010.

Winter often brings hen harrier to the area along with short-eared owls. It even has records of rarer birds like lesser grey shrike, corncrake, quail, spotted crake, ruff, wood and pectoral sandpiper, garganey, common crane, osprey, rough-legged buzzard and honey buzzard. Breeding waders add to the summer months along with grasshopper warblers and plenty of owls, with all five of the common species having been found breeding in the area in some years.

Botanically, the Carr is not rich but has a mixed list of beetles, molluscs and butterflies, with small skipper continuing its journey north having colonised from the south. Dragonflies use the many ditches on site, attracting hobby to the area. Roe deer is the largest mammal on site, with both otter and mink having been recorded.

This habitat is close to the Big Water Country Park (NZ227734) and is run jointly by the Newcastle Rangers Service and Northumberland Wildlife Trust. There are three hides on site, with one of these open to the public while the other two are for members of the Wildlife Trust. This is a former mining subsidence site creating 50 acres (20 hectares) of open water. The grassland here has old medieval ridge and furrow which supports a wide mixture of plants including pepper saxifrage, smooth tare, wild carrot, great burnet and agrimony.

This area is well known for its bird life and the hides have helped locals identify many species, often on passage, like Caspian, little, black- and white-winged tern, white stork, common crane, jack snipe, red-throated diver, ruddy shelduck, Mandarin duck and white-fronted goose. The areas of willow scrub and alder have attracted firecrest and Coues' Arctic redpoll. A feeding station is a useful site to check for garden birds.

A raft out on the water allows common tern to breed and many duck use the raft to rest. Winter duck includes wigeon, teal, gadwall and shoveler with goldeneye, pochard and tufted duck using the deeper areas to dive for food. The real star in recent years has been otter and this is now one of the best places in the north-east to find this mammal.

To the north of Newcastle is the Gosforth nature reserve (NZ260700) run for the members of the Natural History Society of Northumbria. This area of 150 acres (60 hectares) has been run as a reserve since 1929. It has two hides and a viewing screen and has had nearly 180 species of bird identified, along with a long list of moths, beetles and flora. In recent cold winters bitterns have been a star attraction here, along with otters, but there are many notable species for Northumberland such as water shrew, noctule bat and red squirrel.

Of the plants, the most notable species is coral root orchid. With triffid in its Latin name this species of orchid, its feet firmly attached to a fungus on which it feeds, has attracted attention from botanists for some time. The reserve holds the second largest colony of this plant in England. Two butterflies of note are the white-lettered and purple hairstreak, along with the small yellow wave moth, orange swallow moth and gold spot moth. Varied damselfly and great crested newts also use the reserve area.

The water from the reserve runs into Jesmond Dene. This was originally bought by William George Armstrong and now belongs to the City of Newcastle. It has three miles of pathways and bridges crossing the Ouse Burn. Many exotic trees and plants, especially trees from North America, were added in its early years. Two to look out for are the Spanish sweet chestnut, thought to have been introduced to Britain by the Romans, and Lombardy poplar, from Italy but brought to Britain much later than the Romans.

Native species of plants include lesser celandine, wood anemone and wild garlic. This is a great place to look for the flash of blue as a kingfisher darts along the water, as well as grey wagtails and dipper. Winter often adds the waxwing to the bird list but rarer birds like firecrest and hawfinch have also turned up.

The Roman Fort at Segedunum sees the end of the Hadrian's Wall Path. The remains of the fort here were rescued after houses were demolished over the site. The visitor centre works well for the general visitor but many a walker has found it closed when finishing their long trek. The Rising Sun Country Park (NZ302696) is just two miles north of the Segedunum centre. It has 400 acres to enjoy, with farmland, woodlands, wetlands and open water. It was named after the coal mine here which closed in 1969, leaving 1,180 men out of work and 26 pit ponies redundant.

The park has a centre which was once an isolation hospital. Ironically the hospital was there to treat people with fresh air, exactly as the park does for people today. The mining also left subsidence which adds to the wetlands, especially Swallow Pond, which is the largest area of open water in the park. Birds are one of the main attractions, with water birds a real draw. Several duck, including wigeon, shoveler, gadwall and teal are there in winter, along with gulls dropping in, including Iceland, Mediterranean, little and yellow-legged gull.

Breeding birds on and around the water include mute swan, coot, moorhen, sedge warbler and reed bunting. When black-headed gulls nest in numbers the black-necked grebe occasionally nests with them. Summer visitors like garganey, marsh harrier and spotted crake have passed through, with rarer records of a singing Pallis's warbler, roseate tern and red-rumped swallow. Winter has had Coues' redpoll, waxwing and jack snipe. The farm has open fields and hedges, bringing in yellowhammer, common whitethroat, little owl and kestrel.

A red deer stag has taken up residence in a horse field – when he drops his antlers, there is not much to tell them apart! Where he came from is a mystery, as the wild red deer died out with the Romans, so he could only have escaped from a deer farm. Other mammals include foxes, badgers and hedgehogs. Botanically the farm is very limited, given its industrial past, but both common and marsh orchids are found, along with many common field species of plant.

Dropping back to the Tyne is the North Shields fish quay (NZ364686). This has a history of rare gull sightings, with glaucous, Iceland, Mediterranean, little, Sabine's and even a possible Thayer's gull. It is a wonderful walk or bike ride to Tynemouth from here, along the waterfront with views into the river and onto Black Midden Rocks where more gulls and terns roost along with your first eider duck. Winter waders include both turnstone and purple sandpiper, along with oystercatcher, curlew and redshank.

Tynemouth itself (NZ372692) has a history of bird migration, with a ringing station catching the birds in order to study it. It is thought that a Roman fort was once situated on the headland but only a few stones have been found there, now the site of a castle and priory. The priory was founded in 651 A.D. and the castle built around 1095. Standing on the hill is a present-day statue of Admiral Lord Collingwood, who was second-in-command to Nelson at the Battle of Trafalgar. This replaces a large statue of Hadrian which was thought to have stood here, placing the great emperor in view of every boat entering the Tyne.

In the bushes by the present-day statue, especially in autumn with an east wind blowing, there have been records of eastern birds like yellow-browed, Radde's and Pallis's warbler. On the grass around the statue have been Lapland bunting, shore lark and red-throated pipit. The wooded car park here has held barred warbler, red-breasted flycatcher and firecrest, while down at the base of the priory, dusky warbler, wryneck and Blyth's reed

Tynemouth Castle

Short-eared owl

warbler have been found. Two rare swifts – pallid and chimney swift – have been found here, the latter having come from North America. Seawatching has produced little auk, long-tailed skua, sooty shearwater, Sabine's gull and Bonaparte's gull. Even rare moths have landed here, with silver-striped hawk moth and great brocade.

Reaching this part of the Tyne, birdwatchers cannot help but travel the extra four miles up to St Mary's Island (NZ353754). Here is a seawatching hide along with a managed wetland and scrub for catching rarities. A red-flanked bluetail was a great find here in 2010, with a good mixture of rarer warblers. Large flocks of golden plover and lapwing add to the waders, along with purple sandpiper and turnstone. I have even seen both short-eared and long-eared owls make land after flying across the North Sea from mainland Europe. This Northumbrian coast is famous for its birdwatching and you really need to travel even further north, out of the range of this book, to find more sites like Druridge Bay and Holy Island.

Bolden Flatts (NZ377614) is found on the south side of the river and is a wet grassland where flooding takes place in winter. It covers 84.5 acres (32.2 hectares) of SSSI and was once a racecourse, which probably saved it from development. It has a wide variety of waders and duck using the area in winter and can attract wild swans, including whooper and even Bewick's swans. Some of the unusual birds found here have included woodchat shrike, Egyptian goose, American wigeon and white stork. A mixture of geese has been found, including tundra bean, lesser white-fronted, barnacle, pink-footed and lesser Canada goose.

The winter waders here are often large concentrations of lapwing and golden plover, with redshank, curlew and snipe in smaller numbers, while migrating species include black-tailed godwit, ruff, greenshank, spotted redshank, wood sandpiper and little ringed plover. The water can attract up to 1,000 gulls, with Iceland, glaucous and Mediterranean gull along with commoner species. Wigeon and teal are the most common ducks here in winter. The botanical interest comes from medieval ridge and furrow grassland, with pepper saxifrage, sneezewort, yellow rattle and tubular water dropwort in the wetter areas.

South Shields had the Roman fort of Arbeia, built to protect the mouth of the Tyne and which became the main supply base for all forts along the Wall. Nearby at Jarrow is Bede's World, which looks at history from 650 A.D. with the rise of Christianity in Britain. And don't forget St. Cuthbert and his ducks! He is the first known protector of birds in Britain.

South Shields also has the Leas. This is an area of greenbelt land owned by the National Trust stretching 5–6 miles south along the coast into Whitburn coastal park, with the Souter lighthouse open to the public. It has several interesting bird sites on it, including Marsden Rock, where the famous arch fell into the sea in 1996. It is a sea stack standing 300 feet from the main cliffs, built mainly of magnesium limestone, and still home to several thousand breeding sea birds including kittiwakes, cormorants, herring gulls and fulmar. Guillemots and razorbills visit the rock and in recent years the latter have started to breed.

The vast areas of grasslands attract wintering Lapland bunting and occasional shore lark and snow bunting, with areas uncut to allow the birds to find seed (and to save money, of course!) Skylarks are everywhere in this uncut grass, especially in summer, with their song sounding out even across the sea. Seawatching is very good with lots to look at throughout the year. You can watch all along the coast but there is a seawatching hide, run by the Durham Bird Club, three quarters of a mile south of the lighthouse.

Passing terns like Arctic, roseate and sandwich add to the kittiwakes, shearwaters and rarer Sabine's and Bonaparte's gulls and white-billed diver. Common scoter are often joined by velvet scoter and long-tailed duck, while gannets rule supreme in summer, heading back north to breed on Bass Rock in the Firth of Forth. Many whales and dolphins have also been seen from here, including humpbacked and minke whale.

And it is not only seabirds that can be seen from here: many tired migrant birds have made the Leas their arrival point. A small quarry at Trow (NZ383665) made the headlines in 2009 with the first eastern crowned warbler for Britain. Birds like yellow-browed warbler, firecrest, black redstart and barred warbler have been found here. The Leas is classed as magnesian limestone grassland which supports plant communities such as birdsfoot trefoil, yellow-wort, knapweed, harebell and a number of species of orchid, including common spotted, bee and the occasional pyramidal orchid.

Across the road is Marsden Old Quarry local nature reserve (NZ395644) where the increase in vegetation has made it much harder to find these tired migrants. This quarry has a rich history of excellent birds like Richard's pipit, rustic bunting, red-flanked bluetail, red-eyed vireo, Pallas's warbler, wryneck, pallid swift and honey buzzard, to name just a few.

Breeding birds here include both kestrel and little owl. The magnesian limestone grassland here holds several interesting flowers, such as rock rose, small scabious, salad burnet and carline thistle.

On this side of the river a wide range of other nature reserves are run by Gateshead and South Tyneside Councils as well as by the Durham Wildlife Trust. Information can be found on several websites such as Gateshead Birders and on the north side of the river (see Suggested reading and Useful contacts).

102

Carline thistle

Suggested reading

Birds and Wildlife in Cumbria. Annual. The Cumbria Naturalists Union.
Birds in Northumbria. 2005–2009. The Northumberland and Tyneside Bird Club.
Dark, P. 2000. *The Environment of Britain in the first Millennium A.D.*
Fisher, J. 1966. *The Shell Book of Birds.*
Miles, J. 1992. *Hadrian's Birds.*
Miles, J. 2010. *Best Birdwatching Sites – The Solway Cumbria, Dumfries and Galloway.*
Moffat, A. *The Wall: Rome's Greatest Frontier*
Yalden, D.W., Albarella, U. 2009. *The History of British Birds.*

http://www.roman-britain.org/

Useful contacts

Carlisle City nature reserves. Tel. 01228 817200 http://www.carlisle.gov.uk/leisure_and_culture/
   parks_and_open_spaces/nature_reserves.aspx
Carlisle Natural History Society covering Cumbria http://www.carlislenats.org.uk/

Chopwell Forest http://www.forestry.gov.uk/chopwell

Cumbria Bird Club http://www.cumbriabirdclub.org.uk/

Cumbria Wildlife Trust. Tel. 01539 816300 http://www.cumbriawildlifetrust.org.uk/

Durham Bird Club http://www.durhambirdclub.org/dbc.pl/

Durham Wildlife Trust. Tel. 0191 584 3112 http://durhamwt.co.uk/wp/

Friends of Red Kites http://www.friendsofredkites.org.uk/

Gateshead Birders http://www.gatesheadbirders.co.uk/

Gateshead Rangers Service at Thornley. Visitor centre tel. 01207 545212 http://www.gateshead.gov.uk/Leisure%20and%20Culture/countryside/vistorcentres.aspx

Kielder Forest http://www.visitkielder.com/site/things-to-do/wildlife-and-nature

Living Landscapes http://www.livinglandscapesnortheast.org.uk/regionalfocus-hadrian.html

National Trust Souter Lighthouse. Tel. 0191 529 3161 http://www.nationaltrust.org.uk/main/w-souterlighthouse

Natural England Newcastle. Tel. 0191 229 550

Natural England Cumbria. Tel. 01539 792800

Natural History Society of Northumbria – Gosforth Nature Reserve http://www.nhsn.ncl.ac.uk/resources-gosforth-nature-reserve.php

Newcastle Rangers Service, Parks and Countryside. Tel. 0191 265 6439 http://www.newcastle.com/core.nsf/a/rangers

Northern Kites http://www.northernkites.org.uk/

North Tyneside. Tel. 0191 219 2505 for local nature reserves http://www.northtyneside.gov.uk/browse.shtml?p_subjectCategory=646

Northumberland and Tyneside Bird Club http://ntbc.org.uk/

Northumberland Wildlife Trust. Tel. 0191 284 6884 http://www.nwt.org.uk/

Radio tracking birds of prey http://www.roydennis.org/

RSPB Campfield Marsh Reserve. Tel. 01697 351330 http://www.rspb.org.uk/reserves/guide/c/campfieldmarsh/

RSPB Geltsdale Reserve. Tel. 01697 746717 http://www.rspb.org.uk/reserves/guide/g/geltsdale/

RSPB Newcastle office, 1 Sirius House, Amethyst Rd, Newcastle Business Park, NE4 7YL Tel 0191 233 4300

RSPB members group at Carlisle http://www.rspb.org.uk/groups/carlisle/

RSPB members group at Durham http://www.durham-rspb.org.uk/

RSPB members group at Newcastle http://www.rspb.org.uk/groups/newcastle/

South Tyneside. Tel. 0191 424 7423 http://www.southtyneside.info/article/8745/Local-Nature-Reserves

The Bewick Society http://www.bewicksociety.org/index.html

The North Pennines AONB http://www.northpennines.org.uk/

Whitley Castle http://www.english-heritage.org.uk/professional/research/landscapes-and-areas/archaeological-field-survey-and-investigation/whitley-castle/

103

Little Grebe

Visitor centres

(from west to east)

Maryport

Senhouse Roman Museum. CA15 6JD.
Tel. 01900 816168
http://www.senhousemuseum.co.uk/

There is no centre at the end of the Wall, but Senhouse was one of the sea forts protecting the Solway. Future funding may well expand this site.

Campfield

CA7 5AG
Tel. 01697 816300

No centre along the Wall is dedicated solely to the area's wildlife but Campfield RSPB at the end of the Wall may, if funding allows, expand to include a centre.

Caerlaverock WWT

DG1 4RS
Tel. 01387 770200
http://www.wwt.org.uk/caerlaverock

Situated on the north side of the Solway, this is the best centre of all for wildlife.

Tullie House Museum, Carlisle

CA3 8TP

Tel. 01228 618718

http://www.tulliehouse.co.uk/

A Roman exhibition was created here in 2011. There is also a very good wildlife section.

Birdoswald Roman Fort

CA8 7DD

Tel. 016977 47602

http://www.english-heritage.org.uk/daysout/properties/birdoswald-roman-fort-hadrians-wall/

Opening times are limited in winter. Attractions have included a live videocam on a swallow's nest.

Vindolanda

NE47 7JN

Tel. 01434 344277

http://www.vindolanda.com/Home.htm

Digs are taking place on site.

Roman Army Museum

CA8 7JB

Tel. 016977 47485

http://www.vindolanda.com/

Run by the Vindolanda Trust.

Once Brewed

NE47 7AN

Tel. 01434 344396

http://www.northumberlandnationalpark.org.uk/visitorcentres

Housesteads Visitor Centre

NE47 6NN
Tel. 01434 344525
http://www.nationaltrust.org.uk/main/w-vh/w-visits/w-findaplace/w-hadrianswallandhousesteadsfort/

Chesters Fort and Museum

NE46 4EU
Tel. 01434 681 379
http://www.english-heritage.org.uk/daysout/properties/chesters-roman-fort-and-museum-hadrians-wall/

This is the best Roman cavalry fort in Britain, boasting bats in the museum, riverside views and meadow grassland.

Corbridge

NE45 5NT
Tel. 01434 632349
http://www.english-heritage.org.uk/daysout/properties/corbridge-roman-town-hadrians-wall/

This was one of the most prosperous Roman towns close to the Wall, where soldiers went on their days off. This was the limit of boats moving up the Tyne.

Great North Museum, Newcastle

NE1 4JA
Tel. 0191 2326789
http://www.twmuseums.org.uk/

The museum is connected to many of the Roman sites in the north-east. The EYE programme offers you the chance to log records of wildlife in the area.

http://www.ericnortheast.org.uk/eye-project-website.html

Tyne Riverside Park, Newburn

NE15 8ND
Tel. 0191 2648501

107

http://www.newcastle.com/core.nsf/a/tyneriverside

A visitor centre is open here at weekends and at odd times through the week.

Jesmond Dene, Newcastle

NE7 7BQ
Tel. 0191 281 0973
www.jesmonddene.org.uk

A visitor centre is open at weekends and during the school holidays. Pets Corner is open Sunday – Thursday, 10.00–15.45, and on Fridays, 10.00–12.00.

Segedunum Roman Fort, Wallsend

NE28 6HR
Tel. 0191 2369347
http://www.twmuseums.org.uk/segedunum/

The start or end of the Wall!

Rising Sun Country Park

Tel. 0191 6432241
http://www.northtyneside.gov.uk/browse.shtml?p_subjectCategory=523

Thornley Visitor Centre

NE39 1AU
Tel. 01207 545212

Swalwell Visitor Centre

NE16 3BN
Tel. 0191 4142106
http://www.gateshead.gov.uk/Leisure%20and%20Culture/countryside/vistorcentres.aspx

Provides information on the Derwent Valley area of Gateshead.

Arbeia, South Shields

NE33 2BB

Tel. 0191 4561369

http://www.twmuseums.org.uk/arbeia/

The fort protecting the entrance to the Tyne.

Souter Lighthouse and The Leas, Whitburn

Tel. 0191 5293161

http://www.nationaltrust.org.uk/main/w-souterlighthouse

Information and the chance to climb the lighthouse.

Thomas Bewick's birthplace, Cherryburn

NE43 7DD

Tel. 01661 843276

http://www.nationaltrust.org.uk/main/w-vh/w-visits/w-findaplace/w-cherryburn/

A chance to see where the great man lived.

Bede's World

NE32 3DY

Tel 0191 4892106

http://www.bedesworld.co.uk/

A different part of this area's history.

Wren

The Wall month-by-month

January

The Solway is stacked full of geese, with both barnacle and pink-footed found on the English side of the water. Look out for rarer species of geese amongst the flocks, with both snow and red-breasted goose having been found. The higher parts of the Wall are great for raptors, with hen harrier likely along at Grindon Lough. Try Greenlee for otters, while roe deer are out in the open at Geltsdale.

February

Gulls are in big numbers at Newburn and Shibdon. Look out for the white primaries on both glaucous and Iceland gulls. Greater black-backed gulls are searching the rivers for dying salmon. Divers can be found off Tynemouth and Whitburn and check the scoter flocks for signs of velvet scoter. Goshawks start displaying at Kielder.

March

The first signs of spring are often seen in the first flowers like coltsfoot, primrose and lesser celandine. Frog spawn is likely around the ponds while grey herons, along with raven and crossbill, have the first eggs. The first migrants flying in from Africa may well be sand martin and wheatear, while along the high Wall look out for passing ring ouzel and the first curlew returning to breed around Steele Rigg. Kittiwakes return to the quayside of Newcastle to start nest building.

April

This is a better month for butterflies with peacock, small tortoiseshell and comma feeding on the dandelions, and the first orange-tip laying eggs on the cuckoo flower. Migrant birds arrive en masse with the first cuckoo at Walltown Crags, pied flycatcher at Geltsdale and grasshopper warbler at Rayton Willows. Ospreys return to Kielder while common toads start to lay their strings of eggs. Early purple orchids love the rich woodland, with bilberry flower giving early nectar to the bumble bees.

Comma butterfly

May

Birdwatchers gather at Bowness to watch the migration of skuas arriving from West Africa. Many of these same birds fly inland to use the Tyne Gap to head up to the Arctic Circle, along with barnacle geese and many species of wader. Mountain pansy and spring sandwort are already in flower on the Beltingham river gravels. Black grouse are at their best, displaying for hours in an attempt to attract a mate, with birds observed at Geltsdale and Plenmeller.

June

The moors come alive with hatching nestlings of red grouse, meadow pipits, skylarks, curlew, lapwing and redshank. Emperor moths hatch out in the daytime and flutter over the heather with merlin in pursuit. The marshes come into bloom with water avens, water cinquefoil, ragged robin and cotton grass. Damselflies hatch around the edge and dance over the water, little egrets gather at Shibdon Pond and noctule bats hawk over Far Pastures.

July

The upland areas are already losing their birds with curlew heading for the Solway and east coast. Tyne helleborine is at its best along with green-flowered helleborine growing under the beech trees. The silage and hay are being cut on the high ground with flocks of common gulls already arriving from Scandinavia and Russia. Big dragonflies add spice to the wetlands with emperor, southern hawker and red-veined darter new to many areas, especially in Cumbria. Young red kites take to the air around Gateshead.

August

There's more interest on the coasts at this time of year, as the birds leave and the uplands become quiet. Seawatchers at Whitburn see the first sooty shearwaters arriving from the south Atlantic. Adult waders returning from the Arctic still have their summer coats and juveniles often need to be looked at twice. Ducks become ugly as their moult leaves them in yet another plumage. Young grebes no longer need a ride on their parents' backs while wetlands burst with yet more bloom, with hemp agrimony, meadowsweet, purple loosestrife and water mint.

September

Already the first sounds of returning geese can be heard, with the pink-footed first to arrive, followed by the barnacle. Large skeins often enter the Tyne heading west back to the Solway. The woods are alive with fungi: look out for boletus and chanterelle, which are good to eat. Butterflies search for the last nectar on devil's-

Scarlet wax cap

bit scabious and ragwort. Flocks of siskin and redpoll drop to the low ground searching out alder seed.

October

East winds bring the rare migrants to Tynemouth along with woodcock and jack snipe all the way from Russia to Newburn. Most grebes head for the sea and float in with the tide on the Solway along with divers, goldeneye and scaup. Salmon make their way up the smaller rivers with great places to watch them at Lower Gelt and Allen Banks.

November

A great walk takes you around the Rising Sun Country Park looking for duck and farmland birds. Winter swans are still passing through so look out for them around Whittle Dene and Campfield. The last flowering plant is ivy so the final heat of the year adds red admiral and bluebottles. Ducks are in full plumage again and it is worth looking for pintail, shoveler and wigeon on the Solway and Grindon Lough.

December

A trip to the Metro Centre could add some winter gulls if you head back via Shibdon Pond, or willow tit at Far Pastures, feeding on handouts, maybe along with a water rail. Try identifying some trees in Jesmond Dene or Allen Banks. Walk the High Wall looking for ferns or try the Solway Mosses for wintering hen harriers. Look for mammal tracks in the snow or walk on the moors looking for bullfinches and snow buntings.

115

Cuckoo

Britain's bird species in Roman times

The total number of species recorded in Roman Britain, judging from remains found mainly in digs, varies between 94 (Parker 1988) and 136 (Yalden and Albarella 2009). The 136 species includes one or two from Pictish digs dated to this period as the Romans had not conquered those areas. An increase in small bird numbers comes from one site called Ossom's Eyrie Cave, in the Peak District of Staffordshire, where Yalden himself carried out work.

While a good number of these remains were found along the Wall, it is interesting to look at the total as a demonstration of what was found at that time. A map of Roman digs shows that finds were very much concentrated in the south of England, giving a biased view of the distribution of the birds. Given what we know today, many of these species could have occurred this far north but their remains have yet to be found. Only five of the 136 species may have not made it this far north at that time. Sadly, one is now extinct.

Mute swan (*Cygnus olor*)

This bird was found as far north as York but most records are from the south of England. Julius Caesar was amazed that the British tribes felt it unlawful to eat or kill swans. This did not stop the Romans using the swans as food.

Whooper swan (*Cygnus cygnus*)

Single remains found at Carlisle stand as the northern record but due to the effects of the last Ice Age, this bird may have had a more southerly wintering range than the one it has today, with records from the south coast of England. Up to 1,000 birds may winter on the Solway nowadays with anything from a single bird to 200 on the east coast.

Bewick's swan (*Cygnus columbianus*)

This swan is found around York but today is never common this far north, mainly due to milder winters keeping it wintering in Europe. It is occasionally found in whooper flocks on the Solway and along the east coast.

Bean goose (*Anser fabalis*)

This is hard to distinguish from greylag goose but one record has been found at Carlisle. Today it is a declining species in this area with recent regular wintering flocks in south-west Scotland and at Grindon Lough now abandoned. Singles sometimes turn up in pink-footed geese flocks at both ends of the Wall.

Pink-footed goose (*Anser brachyrhynchus*)

This species is found at Carlisle, with modern numbers often in the thousands around the Solway, especially from January to April. Record numbers – up to 42,500 – were found in December 2010. Small numbers are on the east coast north of the Wall around Druridge Bay and may add up to 4,000.

White-fronted goose (*Anser albifrons*)

A single record was again found at Carlisle but this is now a rare bird, with odd ones turning up in other geese flocks. A small group of the Greenland form use the Grindon Lough area. This form is more common in south-west Scotland in winter.

Greylag goose (*Anser anser*)

This was probably the only wild breeding goose found along the Wall in Roman times. Place names suggest that it bred on cliffs, as it still does today, along the River Eden. This species was the main one to be domesticated for food and used as an avian guard dog. Large feral populations now winter at both ends of the Wall, often joined by northern birds from Iceland.

Barnacle goose (*Branta leucopsis*)

This is by far the most common goose to be found at digs around Carlisle. Amazingly, it was also common around York and Gloucester, which suggests that it also wintered on the nearby estuaries of the Humber and Severn. It is unlikely that this was due to trade away from the Solway as its remains would have been common at other sites away from estuaries. The present population on the Solway is around 35,000, having increased from a low of 300 birds due to over-shooting. The bird is now protected by law.

Brent goose (*Branta bernicla*)

A single set of remains of this small goose was found at Carlisle. This bird is more likely to be have been found on the eastern end of the Wall, with a modern-day population of the light-bellied form still found north of the Wall around Lindisfarne, breeding in Greenland and north-east Canada.

Shelduck *(Tadorna tadorna)*

A single set of remains was found at Vindolanda. Only in recent years has this bird started to nest inland in Britain, with Grindon Lough and Whittle Dene having birds in spring. A moult migration takes place in summer with males often flying across the North Sea to Wadden Sea in Germany. Many will use the Tyne Gap, providing more records such as the one found at Vindolanda.

Wigeon *(Anas penelope)*

The wigeon is the third most common duck found in digs. Winter brings large numbers to both ends of the Wall with smaller numbers inland, especially at Grindon. Exceptional numbers are found further up the east coast around Holy Island with up to 6,500 in 2009. Very small numbers breed inland today in black-headed gull colonies.

Gadwall *(Anas strepera)*

This was probably a winter migrant in Roman times as not until 1909 did this species breed in Scotland. Even today gadwall is more of a winter bird in North Cumbria, arriving with wigeon, while it is a regular breeding bird in Northumbria.

119

Teal *(Anas crecca)*

The second most common duck found in Roman digs as well as a common wintering bird at both ends of the Wall. A small breeding population is presently found in the Pennines and on the Solway Mosses.

Mallard *(Anas platyrhynchos)*

This was the most common duck in Roman times as it was domesticated and used for eggs and meat.

Pintail *(Anas acuta)*

This is a very rare breeding bird in Britain today but large numbers – several thousands – come to the Solway each winter from Russia. This is a much rarer wintering bird on the east side of the Wall with only Holy Island having any numbers.

Garganey *(Anas querquedula)*

A migrant from Africa now summering in very small numbers at either end of the Wall. Garganey remains were found as far north as Catterick in North Yorkshire.

Shoveler *(Anas clypeata)*

An uncommon breeding duck at both ends of the Wall but numbers increase in winter, especially on the Solway at Druridge Bay. The nearest Roman remains came from York.

Pochard *(Aythya farina)*

More of a declining winter visitor to Cumbria and Northumbria but odd pairs nest at the east end of the Wall, with two broods found in 2009 at the Rising Sun Country Park, just north of Wallsend. All remains found in the south of England.

Tufted duck *(Aythya fuligula)*

This duck was once only a wintering bird in the UK but now breeds over most of the country, having started around 150 years ago. Remains of this duck were found at York.

Scaup *(Aythya marila)*

This is a winter visitor to the Solway, mainly coming from Iceland, but is a good find on the east coast. There is only one record of this duck.

Eider *(Sometaria mollissima)*

120 No remains of this duck have been found. This is surprising as it was found in earlier Neolithic digs and recorded on the east coast as early as 676 A.D. According to the journal of the Venerable Bede, *Life of St. Cuthbert*, the first bird sanctuary in the world was created by the saint for the eider duck at Holy Island.

Long-tailed duck *(Clangula hyemallis)*

An Arctic breeding bird, nesting no closer than Iceland but wintering mainly in Scotland, with small numbers off the east end of the Wall. Only one set of remains have been found.

Goldeneye *(Bucephala clangula)*

This bird is mainly a wintering bird in most parts of Britain but from 1970 started breeding in parts of Scotland. Summering birds have been recorded in Cumbria.

Red-breasted merganser *(Mergus serrator)*

This is very much a coastal breeding and wintering duck in Northumberland but does move inland, especially to the Lake District in Cumbria to breed.

Goosander *(Mergus merganser)*

The goosander first bred in Britain in 1871, in Perthshire, but it took another 80 years for it to breed in Cumbria. Nowadays it even breeds further south. Numbers increase with the arrival of winter birds from Scandinavia. There were record numbers on the sea in Cumbria in 2011, when inland waters froze, and over 300 were counted. Only one record has been found from the Roman period.

Red grouse *(Lagopus lagopus)*

Only one record came from Corbridge in the Roman period indicating that heather, the main food of the red grouse, was not a common habitat during this period. Today, several thousand can be shot each year on individual moors.

Black grouse *(Tetrao tetrix)*

This was a very common bird during the Roman period but with the management of the uplands for heather came a massive decline. Recent winters have killed many birds on red grouse moors.

Capercaillie *(Tetrao urogallus)*

Remains have only been found at York but the bird may well still have been breeding in the high Pennines and Lake District. A reintroduction was attempted in 1968–1969 in Grizedale Forest, Cumbria with eggs brought down from Scotland. In total, 15 hens and 25 cocks were released but sadly the scheme did not work.

Red-legged partridge *(Alectoris rufa)*

A single set of remains was found in England. This must have been a bird imported into the country as only in recent times has the red-legged partridge been released for shooting purposes.

Grey partridge *(Perdix perdix)*

This was a commonly eaten bird in Roman times, so common that it appears on Roman coins found in Britain. This bird is much rarer nowadays due to changes in agriculture and competition from the introduced red-legged partridge.

Quail *(Coturnix coturnix)*

This is a migrant which arrives here from its wintering grounds in Africa. Both the adult birds and eggs are used for food and kept like domestic poultry. York was the nearest location where remains dating from Roman times have been found.

Pheasant *(Phasianus colchicus)*

There is an ongoing debate about when this species was actually brought to Britain but it was definitely eaten by the Romans, housed like chickens in a cage. A mosaic from Cirencester shows this bird in around 300 A.D. The first written evidence shows that the pheasant was in Britain by 1043 A.D.

Black-throated diver *(Gavia arctica)*

Only a single set of remains was found further south of a bird which is a rare nester in Scotland, with increased numbers arriving from further north.

Great northern diver *(Gavia immer)*

Remains of this diver species have been found further south but it is a winter visitor to our region. Amazingly there have been no records for red-throated diver, which is far more common than the black-throated and great northern diver.

Fulmar *(Fulmarus glacialis)*

The only remains from the Roman period have been found on the Isle of Man.

Manx shearwater *(Puffinus puffinus)*

Found in Pictish digs although, surprisingly not on the English side of the Wall. The name Manx derives from its home on the Isle of Man, only 20 miles from Cumbria as the crow flies.

Gannet *(Morus bassanus)*

A common food on Scottish islands up to the 19th century and, not surprisingly, given its nickname 'Solent goose'. It breeds as close as Scar Rocks in the Solway and Bass Rock on the east coast, from where it gets its Latin name. This bird was found only in Pictish digs around this time.

122

Pelican sp. *(Pelecanus sp.)*

A record of this species from further south may well have been from Dalmatia. The pelican, which was thought to inhabit the fen country in the south, is certainly not a normal Wall species. This is now a very rare bird in south-east Europe.

Cormorant *(Phalacrocorax carbo)*

This bird is still eaten in Iceland and Scandinavia. It has a very big expanding population on the Solway, even ground-nesting away from the normal sea cliffs. It is easy to see at Marsden Rock near South Shields.

Shag *(Phalacrocorax aristotelis)*

The nearest record to the Wall came from the Isle of Man. Today this is a rare bird on the inner Solway, breeding only in Galloway and yet to breed at St.Bees but common on the eastern stretch of the Wall, with large numbers breeding on the Farne Islands.

Bittern *(Botaurus stellaris)*

This bird would have been common in Roman times in the wetlands around the country. Draining nearly drove the bittern to extinction as a breeding bird in the UK, with the removal of reed beds, its main habitat.

Night heron *(Nycticorax nycticorax)*

This was a record from the south of the country, possibly as a summer migrant, as this bird is yet to colonise Britain.

Little egret *(Egretta garzetta)*

Only one record of this bird was found further south. It is unlikely this species was found near the Wall at the time of the Romans, although it was present as a table bird during the Middle Ages. This bird has only recently recolonised the south of England as a breeding bird, starting in 1996 and spreading rapidly as far north as Lancashire, with summering birds found on both sides of the Wall.

Grey heron *(Ardea cinerea)*

This is a very common species now found breeding right across the country with small heronries found at Greenlee and Broomlee Loughs.

White stork *(Ciconia ciconia)*

Only a single set of remains has been found for this very rare bird in Britain, with small numbers migrating across the sea to this country.

Red kite *(Milvus milvus)*

This was once a common bird wherever there was habitation but in the 18th century, the red kite was removed as a breeding bird in much of Britain by shooting estates. Several remains have been found along the Wall.

White-tailed eagle *(Haliaeetus albicilla)*

Remains have been found at Carlisle and at as many as 18 other sites around the country. The last breeding white-tailed eagle was shot in Cumbria in 1791. A reintroduction scheme set up in eastern Scotland has seen birds drift into both Cumbria and Northumberland.

Hen harrier *(Circus cyaneus)*

Remains were found at Ossom's Eyrie Cave in the Peak District. One of the best places to watch this bird in winter is at Campfield RSPB Reserve where it hunts and roosts on the reserve.

Goshawk *(Accipiter gentiles)*

This species can today be seen along the middle section of the Wall as well as at Kielder Forest. Its remains were found further south. It is also a species brought back from breeding extinction in Britain by the release of falconry birds which adapted well to new conifer plantations.

Sparrowhawk *(Accipiter nisus)*

This smaller cousin of the goshawk is today widespread around Britain and would have been common in Roman times.

Buzzard *(Buteo buteo)*

Like the sparrowhawk, the buzzard would have been common in Roman times. Only recently have numbers increased in the eastern parts of the Wall, the bird having been shot out by shooting estates.

Golden eagle *(Aquila chrysaetos)*

Remains of this species were found as close to the Wall as North Yorkshire, as well as at Ossom's Eyrie Cave where it was thought to have nested. Here it was feeding on black grouse with no sign of red grouse remains. In recent years, from 1972–2007, it bred in Kielder Forest and birds were occasionally seen around Spadeadam and the Bewcastle Fells, just north of the Wall.

Osprey *(Pandion haliaetus)*

A record came from a Pictish site and today it can be found in several locations along the Wall, as it probably was during Roman times.

Kestrel *(Falco tinnunculus)*

At one time the kestrel was the most common bird of prey in Britain but it has now been overtaken by the buzzard. A record of this species came from the Isle of Man but it must have been common around the Wall, as it is today, especially at Steele Rigg and Chesters.

Peregrine falcon *(Falco peregrinus)*

Another Pictish record but the peregrine must have been found along the Wall in Roman times as its world distribution is colossal, with some birds migrating from the Arctic to Africa and North and South America.

Water rail *(Rallus aquaticus)*

This is a bird of wet marshes which may have been caught while trying to catch waders and moorhen. It is very secretive during the summer months, while the cold of winter often brings it out into the open.

Corncrake *(Crex crex)*

This is another migrant from Africa now limited to the western islands of Scotland, the Derwent valley in Yorkshire and the fens of Cambridgeshire. This species was once very common in the hayfields of Britain, so may have been common in Roman Britain as modern agriculture expanded.

Moorhen *(Gallinula chloropus)*

A species once used for its eggs and better known as the 'water hen'. Adults are commonly eaten today in the Mediterranean, especially in Portugal, so it has not been a surprise to find it in Roman digs.

Coot *(Fulica atra)*

This too is a species eaten today in the Mediterranean. Large numbers gather together in winter alongside swans, wigeon and gadwall, bringing aquatic vegetation up from the deeper water, helping ducks which do not dive.

Crane *(Grus grus)*

A species found very commonly in Roman digs, with at least 30 locations. This would at that time have been a breeding bird around Britain's wetlands, and records show that as far back as the ancient Egyptians, this species was used for food. The crane also gave rise to many place names around the country.

Great bustard *(Otis tarda)*

This is a southern species with only one record from Roman times. A reintroduction scheme is currently taking place on Salisbury Plain.

125

Oystercatcher *(Haematopus ostralegus)*

Surprisingly, only southern remains have been found for a species which is very common along the Wall. Breeding inland is a relatively new feature for this bird and a nest inside a fort became a visitor attraction in itself in 2011, with two chicks reared. The parents would feed the young only feet away from onlookers, safe in a cordoned-off area.

Avocet *(Recurvirostra avosetta)*

This is another mainly southern species so, not surprisingly, the remains were southern too. In recent years there has been a large increase in the avocet population with pairs spreading north. In 2011 a pair reared young north of the Wall, by the sea at Cresswell Pond, but the bird has yet to breed in Cumbria.

Golden plover *(Pluvialis apricaria)*

Many remains have been found around Roman sites of this bird which can be seen in winter at both ends of the Wall. Breeding golden plover occur on the tops of the Pennines and formerly bred on the Solway Mosses. Some attempt to winter at Grindon Lough.

Grey plover *(Pluvialis squatarola)*

This is a wintering bird at both ends of the Wall, preferring coastal waters, with remains found to the south of the Wall.

Lapwing *(Vanellus vanellus)*

Large numbers of lapwing are winter visitors at both ends of the Wall with a small winter population at Grindon Lough. Breeding birds are also found throughout the region, as would have been the case in Roman times.

Knot *(Calidris canutus)*

This is very much an Arctic bird of the estuaries with varied numbers wintering on the Solway and further north at Holy Island.

Dunlin *(Calidris alpine)*

A very localised breeder of the high Pennines with large numbers using the estuaries in winter having moved down from the Arctic. Occasional birds pass by Grindon Lough.

Snipe *(Gallinago gallinago)*

This is a common breeding bird of wet flushes especially around Sewingshields, with continental birds arriving in the winter, especially on the Solway.

Woodcock *(Scolopax rusticola)*

This was by far the most common wader to be used as food in Roman times. Today it is common along the Wall with satellite tagging revealing that wintering birds arrive from as far away as eastern Russia.

Black-tailed godwit *(Limosa limosa)*

This is more of a wintering bird nowadays with many using the west coast of Africa as they may have done in Roman times.

Bar-tailed godwit *(Limosa lapponica)*

This bird winters on the Solway and around Holy Island and arrives from Arctic Russia.

Whimbrel *(Numenius phaeopus)*

This is a bird which arrives here on passage and only uses the area in spring and autumn, wintering on the west coast of Africa.

Curlew *(Numenius arquata)*

Several birds breed along the Wall around Steele Rigg with many more wintering at both ends of the Wall.

Green sandpiper *(Tringa ochropus)*

This species is a migrant with the majority of birds passing through on migration in spring and autumn. Recent winter records come from Whittle Dean and the River Eden.

Greenshank *(Tringa nebularia)*

Again this is a bird of passage with the majority moving through the area in spring and autumn and wintering in Africa. Only recently have some birds wintered on the coast.

Redshank *(Tringa tetanus)*

This is a bird which would have bred from the coast up onto the fields around the Wall. Large numbers now winter on the coast having arrived from Iceland and Scandinavia.

Turnstone *(Arenaria interpres)*

This was another Pictish record. The turnstone now winters on the coast, especially on the rockier east coast, and partly into the Tyne along the path between Tynemouth and North Shields.

Kittiwake *(Rissa tridactyla)*

The Romans may well have seen this bird on passage along the Wall but remains were found further north of the Wall in a Pictish site.

Black-headed gull *(Chroicocephalus ridibundus)*

This used to be a very common breeding bird along the Wall and is now found at Plenmeller. The Romans would have collected its eggs as they were used in cooking right up until modern times.

Common gull *(Larus canus)*

This is a very rare breeding bird nowadays but it breeds much more commonly in Scotland. The name 'common' derives from the number of birds coming from the continent found on passage and wintering around the area.

Herring gull *(Larus argentatus)*

As with the black-headed gull, eggs would have been collected to use in cooking but adult birds must also have been eaten.

Lesser black-backed gull *(Larus fuscus)*

Small skulls found in digs were thought to be either of this bird or of the herring gull. This bird would have been a summer visitor to the area with most of the population still wintering in the Bay of Biscay. Today there is a large colony of this bird breeding with herring gulls on Rockcliffe Marsh.

Great black-backed gull *(Larus marinus)*

A newly-breeding bird on the Inner Solway with birds arriving from northern latitudes in winter.

Common tern *(Sterna hirundo)*

Remains were found further south but this bird breeds at both ends of the Wall. The remains of a tern species was found at Birdoswald. It may well have been on passage along the Tyne Gap as several tern species have been recorded including arctic, common, sandwich, black, white-winged and little. Common and arctic tern are of a similar size.

Great auk *(Pinguinus impennis)*

How awful to have to write about a species that the Romans may have seen alive but which we sadly never will. Our only sightings of great auk will be the stuffed specimens in the Hancock Museum, Newcastle. Remains of this species were found on the Isle of Man and dated back to A.D. 90.

Guillemot *(Uria aalge)*

A large concentration of breeding birds is found on the Farne Islands, to the east, and at St. Bees on the west, so it is rather surprising that guillemot remains have not been found along the Wall.

Razorbill *(Alca torda)*

Like the guillemot, this bird breeds on cliffs at both ends of the Wall.

Black guillemot *(Cepphus grylle)*

Today this bird is more commonly found north of the Wall with a few isolated breeding sites at St. Bees and west to Galloway. Odd wintering birds are found on the east coast with remains being found south at Filey, Yorkshire.

Little auk *(Alle alle)*

This was a Pictish record of a bird which can arrive in winter in large numbers on the east coast, having been blown down from its Arctic home.

Puffin *(Fratercula arctica)*

This is a species commonly eaten even today in Iceland and Scandinavia, so it might have been expected that more remains would be found. Far more puffins breed on the east of the Wall than the west where today they are quite rare.

Rock dove (domestic) *(Columba livia)*

The Romans enjoyed their pigeon pie and would have domesticated the rock dove. Today it is very hard to find a pure rock dove as so many domesticated pigeons have gone feral and bred with the wild birds.

Stock dove *(Columba oenas)*

This is a bird still found along the Wall using hollow trees, crags and old barns in which to nest. Many remains have been found in Roman sites.

Wood pigeon *(Columba palumbus)*

This is a very common breeding bird today, especially loving to nest in new conifer plantations. Many remains have been found in digs.

Turtle dove *(Streptopelia turtur)*

Sadly, this bird is now very rare this far north, having been very common only 50 years ago.

Cuckoo *(Cuculus canorus)*

When you hear the cuckoo call, the last thing you might think is that you would like to eat it! The Romans, though, thought otherwise and saw the cuckoo as a source of food.

129

Barn owl *(Tyto alba)*

The Romans were very superstitious about owls so it is unlikely that this bird was commonly eaten.

Tawny owl *(Strix aluco)*

Although not found in Roman times, this species was known before and after the Roman occupation. It would have been a common breeding bird during this period.

Long-eared owl *(Asia otus)*

A common breeding bird of today may also have been common in Roman times.

Short-eared owl *(Asio flammeus)*

This bird will have enjoyed open areas created by the clearance of forest and grazing during the Roman occupation, as it does today.

Woodpecker sp *(Dendrocopos sp.)*

With only three species of woodpecker found in Britain, the size of bones may well have shown which species this was. Great spotted is by far the most common today, with lesser spotted much smaller and in decline. Green woodpecker is the largest of the three and may well have lived on ants along the Wall.

Woodlark *(Lullula aborea)*

Larks were a favourite food of the Romans so this present-day, mainly southern breeding species was bound to end up in the pot.

Skylark *(Alauda arvensis)*

Many can be heard around the Wall today, especially around Steele Rigg, as less grazing has allowed safer nest sites for this bird.

Swallow *(Hirundo rustica)*

There were not many barns for swallows to nest in during the Roman period but natural crag nests along the whin sill must have been used.

House martin *(Delichon urbicum)*

The modern-day martin lives in an urban setting but its traditional nest sites may have been on the whin sill along the Wall, as rare crag nesters are still found in Galloway and on the east coast.

Martin sp. *(Riparia/Delichon)*

Either sand or house martins remains were found in the digs. There are big colonies of sand martins at Birdoswald and Chesters while the house martin may have had to use the traditional whin sill to glue its nests to the rock.

Grey wagtail *(Motacilla cinerea)*

A specimen was found in Ossom's Eyrie Cave, Derbyshire.

Wagtail sp. *(Motacilla sp.)*

The remains of a wagtail were found at Birdoswald. The most common wagtail along the Wall today is the pied wagtail, while the yellow wagtail is now a very rare breeding bird turning up at Whittle Dean and Longtown. The grey wagtail is a bird of rivers and streams and can be seen at Willowford and Chesters. The white wagtail is a migrant, moving through the area in spring and autumn.

Wren *(Troglodytes troglodytes)*

Britain's second smallest bird does not make for much of a mouthful!

Dunnock *(Prunella modularis)*

Today this is very much a garden bird, but it may have hung out on the edges of woods in Roman times, with one set of remains found at Birdoswald.

Robin *(Erithacus rubecula)*

The robin, like the dunnock, is today considered tame but back in Roman times it would have been a shy, skulking bird of woodland and scrub, as it still is in Europe.

Redstart *(Phoenicurus phoenicurus)*

Many of these small birds were found in Ossom's Eyrie Cave where conditions preserved their fragile bones for us to find. This is a common breeding bird along the higher section of the Wall.

Whinchat *(Saxicola rubetra)*

This was another find in Ossom's Eyrie Cave. Today it is found in summer, mainly in the moorland areas.

Wheatear *(Oenanthe oenanthe)*

This is a summer breeding bird, especially along the open whin sill. One set of remains was thought to be of the passage bird called the Greenland, bigger than our breeding bird and which moves through in late April/May.

Ring ouzel *(Turdus torquatus)*

This is a summer migrant, also called the mountain blackbird. The bird is still shot in Spain and Morocco for food.

Blackbird *(Turdus merula)*

'Four and twenty blackbirds baked in a pie' goes the nursery rhyme, thought to date from around 1800 but which may well have been dreamt up by the Romans as they loved eating blackbirds.

131

Fieldfare *(Turdus pilaris)*

A larger blackbird for baking in a pie! This is a winter visitor to the Wall from Scandinavia with very small numbers staying to breed occasionally.

Song thrush *(Turdus philomelos)*

This is mainly a summer migrant to the middle section of the Wall, wintering on low ground in Britain and Ireland.

Redwing *(Turdus illacus)*

This is only found around the Wall in the winter months as a migrant from Iceland and Scandinavia. Rare records of breeding were at Spadeadam in 1981 and Geltsdale in 2009.

Mistle thrush *(Turdus viscivorus)*

The 'storm cock' loves the wild ground around the middle Wall but is also found on low ground.

Whitethroat *(Sylvia communis)*

This is another record from Ossom's Eyrie Cave. It is nowadays a common bird on lower sections of the Wall, especially along the Solway. Another warbler species was found in the cave but not identified. Many species of warbler are found in the area of the Wall, all coming here in summer.

Spotted flycatcher *(Muscicapa striata)*

This is another summer visitor to the Wall. Its remains have been found in the cave at Ossom.

Blue tit *(Cyanistes caeruleus)*

Yet another record found in the cave and common throughout Britain.

Great tit *(Parus major)*

Yet another record found in the cave.

Treecreeper *(Certhia familiaris)*

A typical woodland bird found throughout the British Isles with remains found in Ossom's Eyrie Cave.

Great grey shrike *(Lanius excubitor)*

Of the grey shrikes, this is the species most likely to have been found in the dig. This is a winter visitor from Scandinavia while the lesser grey comes up from the Mediterranean region and is very rare in the UK today. It is sparsely found, mainly in the big conifer woods along the Wall, often feeding on goldcrests and small rodents.

Jay *(Garrulus glandarius)*

A very intelligent family, these crows may well have been kept as pets as, like their big cousin the raven, they have the ability to speak.

Magpie *(Pica pica)*

Well known at the east end of the Wall as it is the mascot for the Newcastle United football team.

Jackdaw *(Corvus monedula)*

Jackdaws are nowadays known for using chimney stacks to nest in but the whin sill would have been a common nesting area, as it still is today around Steele Rigg.

Rook *(Corvus frugilegus)*

Once known as crow pie, many of these birds, especially the young, were eaten even up to modern times.

Carrion crow *(Corvus corone)*

Carrion crows were probably eaten, as rooks were, but as they do not nest in colonies they would have been less liable to be caught in numbers. The hooded crow is now found as a breeding bird in northern and western Scotland but a population in the Isle of Man has only recently been taken over, via hybridization, by carrion crow. The hooded crow is also a migrant, flying over from Scandinavia onto the east coast.

Raven *(Corvus corax)*

One of the most common remains found in Roman times but thought to be because it was kept as a pet, rather than for eating. Place names with their roots in the raven's name are widespread in Britain, with Great Corby being the best example close to the Wall.

Starling *(Sturnus vulgaris)*

Millions arrive from Europe to winter here in Britain. The starling was once a common breeding bird, especially in the countryside, but is now declining.

House sparrow *(Passer domesticus)*

A bird closely associated with human settlements.

Chaffinch *(Fringilla coelebs)*

This is a very common bird breeding around the Wall.

133

Greenfinch *(Carduelis chloris)*

This is not as common as chaffinch but is found in particular around modern towns and villages.

Lesser redpoll *(Carduelis cabaret)*

This is yet another find from the Ossom's Eyrie Cave. This bird is common around alder and birch woodland. Winter sees the arrival of continental birds which are slightly bigger than this species.

Common crossbill (?) *(Loxia curvirostra)*

The main species of crossbill are adapted to feed in certain conifer trees, with the size of the bill dictating a preference for certain conifer cones. Common crossbill today enjoys spruce, not found in Roman times, and two-barred crossbill likes larch, which was also absent at that time. Parrot crossbill prefers Scots pine. The main overlap is between common and parrot, so the smaller bill in this case, along with the tree type, may well mean that the remains are that of a common crossbill.

Bullfinch *(Pyrrhula pyrrhula)*

The list of small birds would have been very much reduced were it not for the work carried out in Ossom's Eyrie Cave. This bird is common in the area, actually moving up to heather areas to feed on the seed in winter.

Yellowhammer *(Emberiza citronella)*

Everybody loves to see this beautiful bird and hear its classic song: 'A little bit of bread and no cheese!'

Bunting sp. *(Emberizidae sp.)*

The corn bunting has a large bill for feeding on bigger seeds, so a smaller bill may well indicate the reed bunting, which is common around the Wall today.

134